# Getting Along

## Skills for life-long love

Christopher & Anne Ellinger

Copyright © 2013 by Christopher & Anne Ellinger
All rights reserved

Belmarlin Press

Printed in the United States

ISBN-13: 978-1492333852
ISBN-10: 1492333859

Cover illustration and design by Dana Martin
Interior illustrations by Donna Cohen and Puneet Syal

# Table of Contents

*Acknowledgments*   i
*Introduction*   iii

**Chapter 1: Get ready**
| | |
|---|---|
| Common concerns | 1 |
| Beliefs matter | 3 |
| Stages of skill-learning | 4 |

**Chapter 2: Step out of upsets**
| | |
|---|---|
| Basic commitments | 11 |
| Win-win problem solving | 17 |
| Pattern interruption | 21 |
| The Glitch Process | 26 |

**Chapter 3: Grow through compassion**
| | |
|---|---|
| Appreciation | 33 |
| Empathy | 40 |
| Helping each other change | 43 |
| Healing the sources of pain | 48 |

**Chapter 4: Make decisions wisely**
| | |
|---|---|
| Repetitive decisions | 59 |
| Tricky decisions | 61 |
| Weighty decisions | 65 |
| Agreement-check | 68 |

**Chapter 5: Hot topics**
| | |
|---|---|
| Sexuality | 75 |
| Money | 91 |
| Parenting | 103 |
| Aging together | 111 |
| Working Together | 121 |

*Closing*   135
*Resources*   139

# Acknowledgments

We are grateful for the substantial help from many friends: Dina Friedman for major editing, Ann Davis for assisting in re-writing the introduction, Pinal Maniar and Puneet Syal for all the late night layout sessions of the manuscript, Dana Martin for the beautiful cover illustration and design, and Tonia Pinheiro for proofing. We also appreciate the enthusiasm and thoughtful comments of many other friends, including Amber Espar, Audrey Beth Stein, Betsy & Gail Leondar-Wright, Jonathan Stein, Michele Robbins, Richard Pendleton, Rob Kanzer, and Will Parish.

We acknowledge the many teachers who taught us formative personal growth and communication models. These include: Marshall Rosenberg for Nonviolent Communication, Jeannie Newman for adult educational design, various trainers from Movement for a New Society and Haymarket People's Fund for group facilitation, Harvard Negotiation Project and the Cambridgeport Problem Center for conflict mediation training, Cherie Brown and the National Coalition Building Institute for diversity training, Ellen Deacon and Pamela Haines for Re-evaluation Co-counseling, Sandra Boston for Parent Effectiveness Training, Tom Yeomans for Psychosynthesis counseling, and Stephen Josephs for Neuro-Linguistic Programming (NLP).

We also appreciate our teachers in improvisational music, drama, and dance forms, including Jonathan Fox and Jo Salas for Playback Theatre, Randy Newswanger, Cynthia Winton-Henry and Phil Porter for Interplay, Thomas Cobb and the men's group for SpiritSong, Rhiannon for improvisational song, Martin Keogh, Angie Hauser, and others for contact improvisation dance. Finally, we extend gratitude to Anne's parents, Jan and David Slepian, whose gusto for life and love inspired us.

# Introduction

**Staying in love**

Falling in love is one of life's most desired experiences, without which our time on earth can seem a long slog across a lonely desert. Staying in love, however, is usually less poetic. It's more work than wonder, particularly if you live and work together as we have. How do you keep the mystery of romance alive if there's precious little space between you for any mysteries at all?

In 1981, when we first discovered the pleasure of being together, we forged a commitment not only to stay together, but also to work together to make the world a better place. We were long on idealism and painfully short on experience.

**Bigger than just the two of us**

Somehow, we did it. During our run of three decades, we have not only stayed together happily but also contributed to the world as a couple. In the 1990s, we created a journal called *More than Money* to stimulate new conversations about money, values, and ethical choices. This evolved into Bolder Giving, a nonprofit that promotes inspiring stories of people from across the economic spectrum who give far beyond the norm.

For years, most of the work was an uphill battle, relatively unacknowledged and under-funded. But now we can truthfully say that these two projects are helping to change the national conversation around giving and unleashing untold millions in charitable dollars. Our book, *We Gave Away a Fortune*, won an American Book Award and, after the difficult start-up years, Bolder Giving received breakthrough recognition from the Bill and Melinda Gates Foundation enabling its impact to soar.

We have now passed these beloved projects to the leadership of a new generation of philanthropists. We've gone on to build other social entrepreneurial projects that make our hearts sing: True Story Theater, which fosters community-building and healing through improvised performances of important real-life stories, Playback North America, a network to strengthen this kind of theatre across the continent, and Arts Rising, which promotes participatory arts and social change.

**Relying fully on each other**

Never could we have accomplished any of this without each other's daily involvement and support. We assisted each other through the daily drudgery and the most challenging times: when colleagues in the philanthropic world seemed to think we were just too weird, when we received a shocking rejection from an organization we fostered, and when our first child died at birth. (Happily, our beloved son Micah was born healthy a year later.) Through it all, we managed to keep living, working and loving each other.

**What's your secret?**

Decades ago, when we had been together a mere ten years, some friends asked, "How do you get along so well? Would you tell us your secret?" We responded by putting together *Getting Along*, a sheaf of photocopied pages containing our best relationship tools. We shared that compilation with many friends through the years and were gratified to hear how useful many people found it.

Twenty years passed: time spent raising our son, developing the projects described above, honing the skills we described in the original guide and inventing many more. We decided it would be exciting to cull the lessons we learned since that first writing and put them more attractively into the world with the benefit of electronic publishing. *Getting Along* is now the book you hold, which includes revised and further-developed pieces from our original work plus reflections on the hot topics of sexuality, money, parenting, working together, and aging.

We hope the curious mix in this guide offers a unique and useful window into long-term relationships. It's unusual to find in one book: step-by-step instruction in strengthening your communication, guidance for making tricky decisions, practical advice about money, tips on sexual exploration, antidotes to boredom in long-term relationships… yet all this and more is the territory of a shared life.

**Worth the risk**

We felt shy when we started writing this, aware that we were exposing the idiosyncratic workings of our life together. After all, we didn't create these tools for others; we developed them for our own relationship's needs. But we believe in shared learning and in taking risks, and so the potential gain from sharing our experience seems well worth the slight embarrassment.

We believe that everyone deserves abundant love and skillful support, whether they are simply building a fulfilling partnership or aspiring to offer additional gifts to the world. Our hope is that the skills in this book help you, dear readers, to strengthen all your relationships and to further your creative dreams.

Warmly,
Anne & Christopher

P.S. We are eager to know which parts of this guide you find most useful. After you have read some of it, please take a moment to give us your feedback and to share your own favorite practices. We would be delighted to learn from you. You can reach us via the website, GettingAlong.Us

# Chapter 1
Get ready

# Chapter 1: Get ready

## Common concerns

You may be skeptical that communication skills can help in your particular situation. What works for some people is not always the right thing for others. However, if you have doubts like some of these examples below, we're hoping you may be pleasantly surprised by how useful some of these tools here will be to you.

**My partner doesn't like to "process"**

Many people have had painful experiences with "processing" in relationships. They might equate processing with talking through conflicts endlessly and fruitlessly, with being criticized under the guise of "being honest," or with stuffing genuine feelings to fit some manipulative self-help model. If that's the case, please know our intention is for the exercises to support genuineness.

**I don't like structure**

Sometimes, people don't like "processing" because they prefer other modes than talking, and they assume processing means words, words, and more words. Please adapt the exercises here to fit your individual learning styles. You can draw pictures, write instead of speaking, go for walks, cuddle, or stretch while talking, dance or act out your answers instead of speaking. Be creative!

Many people reject structured communication as too stilted or constraining. We agree that structure for its own sake is pointless; if you are doing fine without structure you probably don't need it! But if your relationship has recurring conflicts, or you feel less than fully heard and appreciated by your partner, then trying these new ways of communicating may help. Even if you have no communication "problems," taking time to explore new tools and models—especially if both of you practice them—can bring fresh ease, delight, and depth to your relationship. As you get good at using them the structure falls away and new ways of relating become increasingly natural.

**My partner and I are so different**

Naturally, it's simpler to get along when you have a lot of commonalities. The two of us are nearly the same age, and both Americans from secular Jewish families. We are also compatible in dozens of ways we didn't realize when we got together: from the kinds of movies, music, and food we most enjoy, to our energy levels, sleep rhythms, and ways of processing information. In these ways, getting along has been easy. If your relationship is straddling major differences, such as age, religion, class, race, culture or language, it may be more difficult to create mutually acceptable styles for working out conflict. Yet developing a robust communication toolkit may be even more vital for the long-term health of your relationship.

**Our situation is seriously bad**

Stressful circumstances (such as unemployment, chronic illness, raising a disabled child) make it much harder to get along. Many situations such as abuse or addiction call for more immediate and basic resources than communication skills. Nonetheless, even in difficult circumstances, better communication can help, especially after you've addressed your crisis.

# Beliefs matter

The practices in this guide are based on beliefs about human interaction quite different from the ones the two of us were raised with. Perhaps you, too, were raised with assumptions like these:

> *It is not okay to ask directly for what you want.*
> *Most emotions are disturbing and bad.*
> *To make someone change, criticize or punish them.*
> *In conflicts there are winners and losers.*
> *People are the way they are; you can't change them.*

In contrast, the models we work with are based on these beliefs:

> **Ask for what you want:** *Discerning what you want and directly requesting it is essential for deep and genuine relationships.*
>
> **Emotions are natural:** *Learning to skillfully express feelings can help us heal, experience being vibrantly alive, and communicate more fully.*
>
> **Encourage growth:** *To best change someone's behavior, including your own, use empathy, appreciation, and encouragement.*
>
> **Find win-win solutions:** *In most situations, you can find creative ways to meet everyone's needs.*
>
> **People can change:** *You can skillfully help each other heal from past hurts and grow into your best selves.*

Because the ways of thinking and acting in this guide are developed from these beliefs, to some they may seem quite strange. We encourage you to try them on anyway, and see whether they improve your relationships and wellbeing.

# Stages of skill-learning

Think of a skill you learned that at first felt awkward and frustrating but eventually became easy. Perhaps driving a car... using new software... learning to cook... playing tennis. To learn new communication skills is no different. It takes practice and persistence to get through the early stages.

When we first we tried on new ways to communicate based on the new beliefs above, we often felt stupid and frustrated. So we developed the skill-learning model below to keep up our spirits as we moved through each stage. We hope the model helps you, too. Even in the early stages, we believe the rewards of these new practices can outweigh the discomforts.

---

### Stages of constructive skill-learning

**Stage 1: Accept confusion:** In this first stage, you're often frustrated, not sure you even understand the basics. Remember this is totally natural. Expect it and don't be thrown.

**Stage 2: Celebrate awkwardness:** In the next stage, you know what you're trying to do but it often seems terribly belabored. Instead of quitting, you can congratulate yourself for reaching the awkward stage.

**Stage 3: Relax into deliberateness:** Now you can do the new skill, but only with concentration. Sometimes you remember the new behavior and sometimes you slip into the old. Again, there's no need to berate yourself when you lose it. Just know it's a normal part of the "deliberate" phase.

> **Stage 4: Notice the new normal:** Suddenly, you're using the skill without even noticing. It just seems natural! Notice how you've changed, so you can appreciate the work you've put into it.

We recommend you to start by practicing the new skills in this guide in relaxed situations. Even skills that appear simple can be tricky when you're upset—which, ironically, is when you need them the most. If it's touchy to practice with your partner, then recruit a friend to try them with you. Give yourself easy successes to start. Then work up to trying them in more tense times.

At first you might chafe against sounding "fake." Don't worry: the more you practice, the more flowing and natural these new ways of communicating will become.

Ready? Let's jump in!

# *Get ready: key points*

### Common concerns

My partner doesn't like to process
I don't like structure
My partner and I are so different
Our situation is seriously bad

### Constructive beliefs

Ask for what you want
Emotions are natural
Encourage growth
Find win-win solutions
People can change

### Stages of skill learning

Accept confusion
Celebrate awkwardness
Relax into deliberateness
Notice the new normal

# Chapter 2
## Step out of upsets

# Chapter 2: Step out of upsets

## Basic commitments

To get along in any relationship, you need constructive ways to respond when you are *not* getting along. You'll be hugely helped by building a toolkit your partner shares: mutually agreed-upon language, concepts and processes that enable you to constructively resolve your differences without spiraling into big scenes or simmering into unexpressed resentments.

The skills in this section were mind-blowing to us when we first practiced them. Anne grew up in a "nice" family where open conflict was avoided at all costs; Christopher's was similar, except that at random times his father would explode in anger. Neither of us really knew how to work things out. Luckily, we both were excited to learn the personal growth and relationship communication concepts and skills below, so different from our upbringing.

If your partner is resistant to trying these new ideas, don't worry. They can revolutionize your relationship even if only you take them on. As the saying goes, it takes two to tango. Listen open-mindedly to what's behind your partner's reluctance. Give it time. Find friends who are interested and practice with them. Another great way to practice is to use the conflicts and upsets you have with yourself! Integrating even one of the practices into your relationship can bring greater ease and connection.

### Say yes to conflict, no to drama

In order to use the tools in the section, you have to be willing to step out of your upsets. This doesn't mean sweeping issues under the rug or denying your feelings; it means letting go of high drama, unnecessary storm and thunder.

If you are someone who is attached to passionate fights for their energy and emotion, if fighting is how you feel alive and cared for, you might be afraid that letting go of your upset means your needs won't get heard.

But fights and conflict are not the same. While you may feel that fights are the most direct way to honestly communicate when you're in emotional pain, they are often not the most productive way to resolve conflict. Far too often, fights leave scars that are sadly unnecessary.

If you're accustomed to feeling close through fighting and making up, resolving conflicts peaceably may feel foreign and even dull at first. But relationships without dramatic upsets can still be full of great vitality and intimacy. Addressing conflict in your relationship offers a potential treasure chest of growth for you and your partner.

Letting go of upsets enables you to embrace conflict more readily when it arises. Instead of just fighting, you can actually hear each other, even when expressing deeply painful feelings. And through skillful listening, you can help each other meet the needs that are causing the upset.

### Choose a good time

It takes physical and emotional energy not to get swept into the other person's upset. It takes energy to listen accurately, to step out of yourself and empathize, and to be creative about solutions. Good timing makes an enormous difference. Often, attempts to resolve conflict go badly because neither partner has sufficient resources of spirit and energy at that time. If you and your partner are tangled in upset feelings and together you don't feel resourceful enough to deal with them well, then STOP. It might feel hard to resist fighting, but STOP until you can get the resources you need.

If you ask to postpone an important discussion until a better time, reassure your partner you are committed to processing together soon:

> *You know, I see you're really upset about this, and I do want to talk it over with you, but right now my head aches and I'm so tired and all I can think about is getting to bed. Can we talk about it in the morning? I could talk after dinner tomorrow, too, if we need more time.*

Or perhaps instead of postponing, you can ask for something that will give you the emotional slack you need:

> *Before we launch further into this, could we spend five minutes remembering some of the fights we used to get into but have successfully worked through? I need to feel more hopeful before taking on this challenge.*

> *Could we have this discussion while we walk outside? I think seeing the beautiful fall leaves will help me listen better.*

> *I bet if I first took a 15 minute run, I'd handle this upset a whole lot better.*

> *Could you wait for me to shower and change my clothes? I promise I'll make time to talk afterwards.*

> *I know this is an important issue for us to work through. But I feel raw and tired from all the difficult talks we've had lately. Would you have the slack to rub my feet for 5 minutes while we're just quiet and listening to some soothing music? I need to feel better connected with you and myself before we take on another hard issue.*

In order to agree to postpone, your partner may need:

- Reassurance that you're committed to addressing the issue.
- Explanation of why taking a break or doing something else will help.
- A chance to vent feelings for a few minutes first. Ask your partner to vent using sounds instead of words, so you don't get caught into the content.
- Help thinking about constructive things to do with upset feelings while waiting for you (e.g. write about her feelings; do something to help her feel more resourceful, too).
- A track record of following through on what you say you'll do (if you ask to postpone).

## Frame a positive context

Before digging into the work of cleaning up upsets or resolving disagreements, give voice to those words that will support you and your partner to be your best selves with each other. Then, instead of being afraid of conflict and trying to avoid it, or falling into an old habit of scarring fights, you both may actually learn to welcome it.

> *Before we launch into discussing our conflict, I ask that you take a deep breath and remember a few things: Remember that I love you, and that I'm committed to taking to heart what you need and finding solutions that serve us both. Remember that we have gotten through difficult things before, and that we have excellent resources to get through whatever is before us now. I trust that working on these issues will teach us to better meet each of our needs and strengthen our partnership.*

Aaah! Hearing any words like these – even one sentence!—in the midst of a painful conflict can help both parties sigh with relief.

## Take brief turns

Here's a common difficulty: you're trying to work out a disagreement, but instead you both keep upsetting each other. Each phrase one of you says ticks the other off, making it hard for the other person to listen. It's like you're both in a slippery dark barrel, and each time you try to crawl towards the light you slip back.

When you both are upset at the same time, the first step is for one of you to say, "Stop! Let's take turns." Then follow this process:

The person speaking is the one whose needs are on the table. The listener is the helper.

Set a timer. Each turn needs to be short enough that the listener can stay in the listening role and not get drawn into the content. Start with 30 seconds each. Then one minute each. Then go to two minutes each. Then five minutes each. By then, perhaps one of you will feel calm enough to do some real listening.

The person more upset talks first. Then switch. You can go back and forth as many times as needed.

**The speaker's job:**

If you have a lot of pent up emotions, you might take the first turn or two to release them. Use sounds instead of words. Sounds are more expressive and far easier for other person to listen to without getting reactive. "Grrrr! GRRRRR!!!"

Speak about yourself, not your partner. Name your own feelings and needs. "I feel irritated! I need rest." Not: "You're mean. You're noisy and inconsiderate!"

Beware of starting a sentence with "I feel you..." That's likely to be a projection onto the other person or a judgment of him, not a feeling. Describe your partner's behavior without labeling him. Give specific observations not interpretations. "When you left dishes in the sink last night," instead of: "when you don't want to be bothered washing up."

**The listener's job:**

If you're just learning this skill or feel really triggered, don't say a word while listening. If you've practiced a lot and are reasonably calm, you can encourage the speaker with empathetic sounds or phrases.

Keep breathing. Try to keep your face as relaxed and accepting as possible. Remember this is a hurting person whom you love.

Let your partner's sharp emotions "roll off your shoulders," not cut into your mind and body. Remember that even if he is blaming you, the speaker is responsible for his own upset, just as you are the one responsible for yours.

Notice what gets you triggered. Name your feelings to yourself as they bubble up, but don't blurt them out.

Stay attentive to the hurting person. If you get too caught up in your own feelings and needs, ask to switch roles.

Be patient. It may take a few rounds of this for you to discern the real needs beneath the upset. Even if it feels emotionally strenuous, keep the faith that this process is quicker and more effective than emotional fights, or leaping to "solutions" by pretending irrational feelings aren't there.

At all times, you need to know whose needs are on the table. It can't be both of you simultaneously. Don't get into problem solving together until you've done enough short back-and-forth that you can really listen. If you start interrupting each other, go back to timed turns. Once both of you are calm and feel fully heard, you might try the problem solving method described next, to come up with creative ways to meet both of your needs.

## Win-win problem solving

In our haste to "fix" a problem, it's easy leap to solutions before we may actually understand the nature of the problem. Then we're resentful that our well-intentioned help was shot down and we're discouraged from offering further ideas.

The first skill in creative problem solving is being willing to not know the answer, but instead to patiently listen as different pieces of the problem become clear. Only when each person's needs are thoroughly understood can you design a solution that creatively satisfies everyone's needs. You have to let yourself trust that such a "win-win" resolution is possible, and not give in to the urge to settle quickly by compromise. Compromises often lead to lingering resentments, because in compromising you give up some of what you want or need. When a win-win solution has been implemented, all the important needs are satisfied and there is nothing left to resent. The "problem" has been transformed into an opportunity to better understand both yourself and your partner.

Here's how the process works:

18 | Getting Along

> **Win-win problem solving:**
>
> Step 1: Listen to both of your needs.
> Step 2: Brainstorm creative ways to meet the needs.
> Step 3: Synthesize a proposal and work out concerns.
> Step 4: Try your solutions for a while; then evaluate.

For example, many arguments start like this: each person expresses feelings indirectly, labels each other, and leads with solutions that seem to be direct opposites.

> *Diane: Christine, why do you always want to read just as we go to bed? You only think of yourself. You know your reading keeps me up! Besides, you'll be grumpy in the morning from lack of sleep. Come on, turn out the light and snuggle with me.*

> *Christine: Nagging me doesn't make me want to snuggle. I so enjoy reading in bed before sleep. Just close your eyes, ignore the light, and you'll be asleep in no time.*

### Listen to both of your needs

The first step of constructive problem solving is to talk about each of your specific needs, leaving solutions aside for the moment. Here is an abbreviated example:

> *Diane: Please tell me what's important to you about reading in bed.*

*Christine: Well, it's about the only time all day that feels like it's just for me. After reading for fifteen minutes I can go right to sleep, but if I try to sleep without it, my mind goes round and round about unfinished work and hassles of my day. I like reading in bed more than other places because it's cozy and warm, and it has the best light—and also, because I get to be close to you!*

Diane first tells Christine what she understood of Christine's experience. Then she asks Christine to listen to her feelings.

*Diane: I feel hurt when you crawl into bed and grab a book. I imagine you're avoiding me. I want to snuggle and talk about our day. It's hard for me to sleep while you read, and not just because of the light, either. Every time you turn the page, it wakes me up. You say you need only fifteen minutes, but sometimes you read for over an hour, and then I have to deal with your grumpiness the next morning.*

## Brainstorm options

Once you understand all the component needs, brainstorm together lots of possible solutions that might meet the needs. For now, refrain from reacting (even with your facial expression) to any of the ideas. Just generate lots of them. Be silly and make each other laugh. Crazy ideas help loosen your minds to new possibilities.

Diane and Christine's idea list:
- *D. wear earplugs.*
- *C. read in living room.*
- *D. come to bed after C. has read 15 minutes*
- *C. snuggle and talk with D. for 10 minutes before reading*
- *D. do the dishes more often so C. can read after dinner.*
- *Buy a warm quilt to make for cozy reading in living room*
- *C. set a watch beeper and stop reading after 15 minutes*
- *Instead of reading, C. listen to story tapes using earphones.*
- *C. read short stories instead of novels; stop at end of one story.*
- *D. knit and listen to music with earphones while C. reads*
- *C. plans how to be cheerful the next day, if reads over 30 min.*

## Synthesize a proposal

After generating lots of possibilities, both partners can discuss which suggestions might work for them, and together work up a proposal. There's no need to talk about solutions that either party rejects. If there aren't enough attractive options, brainstorm some more.

> *Diane: I'd be willing to try knitting and listening to music while you read. Or coming to bed after you've read a while.*
>
> *Christine: I'd actually like help to stop reading after fifteen minutes. I never set a timer because I didn't want to wake you! I'd love to snuggle and talk after reading, as long as we went to sleep within ten or fifteen minutes.*

## Evaluate

At a determined point in the future, discuss how the solutions are working. If the solutions aren't satisfying all the needs (as many will not because the real needs may require more exploration), simply go back into problem-solving mode, taking the new information into account.

> *Diane: I feel hopeful about this plan. Let's try it this week and talk again on the weekend to see if we want to change anything.*

# Pattern interruption

Sometimes we get "triggered" by certain ways our partner holds or expresses himself—a certain tone of voice, a tense holding of the jaw. Anything that will interrupt those automatic triggers will help break the tension. Together, try out different ways to jiggle the energy between you and notice which actions work the best. Below are some suggestions to get your started.

## Play with body habits

Sometimes when dealing with a minor conflict, simply making a change in your body or voice can help you both lighten up. See what it's like to continue the discussion while:

- *Talking back to back or leaning against each other*
- *Standing on chairs*
- *Making your voices extra high or low pitch*
- *Talking in accents*
- *Making strange faces*
- *Talk with your faces scrunched up*

Laughter is great!

## Reverse roles

Sometimes you and your partner may feel locked into opposite positions on an issue. You may be dismayed to find that talking about it doesn't lessen the differences; in fact, the more you talk about the issue, the more polarized you become, until the discussion starts to feel very repetitive. "Ucch! When I say this, you always say that."

A powerful way to reverse this polarization is to literally reverse the positions that you've each taken. For a mutually agreed-upon period of time, you and your partner each pretend that your position is now what the other person was previously advocating. For the role reversal to work, you have to play the new role as honestly as you can, without the least bit of mockery. Remember that this is just an exercise. You don't have to agree with the part you are playing for this period of time. Just be true to it.

Reversing roles can relieve tensions, deepen your understanding of each other's perspective, and loosen your positions by allowing you to voice unexpressed parts of yourselves. Playing opposite roles can turn a struggle against each other into a fun way to reach together for mutual understanding.

There are many ways to play with role reversals. You can try switching roles just for just a few minutes, or you can decide that for several days you will express each other's positions on an issue instead of can your own. You can choose to make your role reversals as genuine and accurate as you can, or you can play with them through light-hearted exaggeration. For example, if you rarely initiate love-making, in a genuine role reversal you might now say, "Let's make love tonight, okay? I miss being close to you," and your partner, the one who always initiates, now acts reluctant. "Oh dear, I really have work to do..." Or to help shift tensions, you could agree to add playfulness and drama to the role reversal. "Darling! I must have you! Now! Yes here, on the kitchen table..." "I think I'd like a few months of celibacy, OK?" Play with it! After the reversals, talk about how they felt and any insights you gained.

We used role reversals during a touchy period when Anne wanted to get pregnant but Christopher wanted to wait. The situation was tense. We switched roles for a few days, playing it up big. Christopher would say, "Beloved, when you get home, I'll have picked out possible names for our baby!" Anne would demur. "Honestly, I don't think I'm ready!" After a few days of playing with this role reversal, we were able to have a much more productive discussion about the decision, each feeling looser about our positions.

## Own responsibility

At the start of an argument, take responsibility for whatever truth is in your partner's accusations, as soon as you can. This can be a dramatic way to interrupt your pattern. "It's true, I was the one emptying the dish drain when your favorite mug fell. I want to do something about it. Can I replace it or reimburse you?" Just step over your defensiveness and do it. After you have taken responsibility, your partner will be more open to discussing extenuating circumstances. "You know, I've been asking the family for weeks to not to pile more dishes in the drainer once it's full. And when your mug fell, the baby was crying and I was carrying her. She was the one to knock it out of the drainer."

It may feel like swallowing pride, but this simple act will eliminate many hours of unnecessary fighting. "Yes, I was late." "It's true, I did raise my voice." "You're right, I wasn't thinking about you when I made that appointment." Take responsibility first, and then discuss the rest of the situation.

## Forgive

Another powerful way to interrupt a pattern of upset or resentment is by asking for or offering forgiveness. "I'm sorry if I hurt your feelings by my grumpiness today. Will you forgive me?" or "I forgive you for hurting my feelings this morning." Initially, your partner may feel uncomfortable: "Don't apologize, I don't think you did anything wrong," or "Don't blame me, I didn't do anything wrong." You can explain that the point is not blame, but to help you both feel that your hurts and needs count.

Paradoxically, asking for forgiveness can be healing in situations where you feel judgmental toward your partner. "I get terribly resentful when you leave your dishes unwashed in the sink, and I really hate harboring those feelings toward someone I adore. Will you forgive me for thinking negatively about you?" Expressing forgiveness can open you both to exploring the deeper issue. If you express forgiveness first before asking, "Can we talk again about kitchen cleanup and each of our needs? I'll make an effort to put aside my judgmental attitudes," your discussion will likely go more easily.

Forgiveness is potent when practiced regularly. You don't need to wait for a special occasion! Assuaging the little hurts means they don't need to build up to a huge issues. Plus it helps to get in the forgiveness habit, so it's less hard to offer in a charged situation.

## Playfully claim the blame

This is especially useful when your partner is in a stew of upset that has nothing to do with you (e.g. bad traffic, a nasty interaction at work, losing her car keys). You playfully claim ALL the blame.

> *Beloved, it's all my fault! I should have protected you better! Please forgive me!*

Often this releases gales of relieving laughter. Your partner's role is to respond,

> *Yeah, you jerk! It's all your fault! Why didn't you know I needed to go to the dentist (even though I didn't tell you I had a toothache) before we left on this vacation?!"*

Why does this work? Often, when we're upset about something we long for someone to blame (even though we know that's not constructive). Often, we blame ourselves but wish we didn't. Or we have the urge to blame our partner, even if the fault was 99% our own. When partners assume more than their share of the responsibility, they are indirectly empathizing with this desire to blame and cutting through any self-blame we have layered on to the already-painful situation.

Note: your partner needs to have read the exercise so she understands what you're doing. Also, you have to sound sincere, not sarcastic. The technique comes from a peer counseling method called "Re-evaluation Co-counseling" that teaches many forms of emotional release. See the Resources section for this and other training in skillful empathy. We also recommend Nonviolent Communication developed by Marshall Rosenberg and Leader (or Parent) Effectiveness Training developed by Thomas Gordon.

## Love the uglies

When we feel angry... depressed... grumpy... upset... most of us not only have to deal with these uncomfortable feelings, but we're also mad at ourselves for feeling and acting that way. We feel ugly and unlovable, which only makes us sink deeper into our bad mood. If, on top of all that, someone we care about criticizes us for our feelings (when we're probably already trying as hard as we can to feel better) it's the opposite of what we need. We desperately need a helpful hand, not a kick.

One way to get out of this downward cycle is to practice "loving the uglies" so the uglies don't scare us. Set aside five minutes to practice with a partner when one of you is in a good mood and the other is down (but not down about you).

> When Al makes an ugly growl, Betsy beams at him with total love and approval. Next Al storms and stomps and Betsy smiles with delight saying "Aw, there must be something you need!" Al snarls, "I hate comments like that!" Betsy beams acceptance, with a gentle "Feeling bad, huh. Must be miserable."

Sometimes you can even talk directly to the uglies. "Hey, you bad mood, let my friend go and stop torturing her." You can develop pet names for each other's favorite uglies, such as "Mr. Anxiety," or "Madam Perfection."

Loving the uglies can help both parties lighten up. Be prepared for laughter and tears: because most of us received disapproval when we felt bad when we were growing up, getting approval now goes deep into the heart.

# The Glitch Process

This is one of the most elegant processes we've come up with. It has saved us from long ugly conflicts many times! However, it is an advanced skill, requiring proficiency both with win-win problem solving described above, and with skillful empathy, described in the next chapter. With practice, "The Glitch Process" may become as quick as the times below, give it ample time when you are first learning it.

Say, George and Francis have been invited to a 6:30pm dinner party. On the car ride there they get upset with each other. They pull up to the house at 6:30 sharp, both fuming. What can they do besides go in and feel hostile all night, or start arguing in the car, where they'll probably end up hopelessly late and still upset?

Luckily, they know the Glitch Process! Here's how it works:

**Step 1: Agree**

They agree to do the Glitch Process. 10 seconds.

> *George: I know we're late for the party but could we please use our glitch process before we go in to feel better connected?*
> *Francis: OK, let's do it! I'm going first!*

## Step 2: Vent

They take turns to each vent strong feelings without using words. Each partner listens without responding. 1 minute each.

> *Francis, weeping: Grrrrr!! (etc.)*
> *George: pounds the steering wheel (etc.)*

## Step 3: Empathize

They make their best guess as to what the other person is feeling and do their best to express it empathetically and genuinely. The other person gives information to help the empathy be more accurate. 3 minutes each.

> *George: Francis, I know you have an intense headache. I bet you wish we didn't have to visit with these folks, is that right? And you could really use some time to yourself? (Francis can add or correct his empathetic guesses.)*
>
> *Francis: I imagine you're bummed because you wanted to get there early to surprise your friends and are frustrated that I wasn't ready when I said I would be? Is that right? (George can add or correct her empathetic guesses.)*

## Step 4: Problem-solve

Based on the needs they heard through empathizing, they come up with creative solutions together about the issue. 2-5 minutes.

> *George: How about I go in now but you rest in the car for a while to ease your headache. Would that help?*
>
> *Francis: I think it would. Then I'll try to enjoy the party for an hour, but if I'm still miserable after that, could we leave without a fuss?*
>
> *George: I can agree to that. I'll make a date to connect with my friends hosting the party another time soon.*

**Step 5: Appreciate**

They express appreciations for each other. 1 minute.

> *Francis, thank you being willing to come, even these aren't your friends. It means a lot to me that we're willing to reach out to them even when you're feeling so bad.*
>
> *George, I appreciate your asking to take this time to process; I feel better. Thanks for being willing to leave early.*

The issue may not feel perfectly resolved, but chances are they both feel a whole lot better. It's probably only about 6:45 (given slack time on each step), just fashionably late, and they're likely to actually enjoy the party.

# *Step out of upsets: key points*

### Basic commitments

Say yes to conflict, no to drama
Choose a good time
Frame a positive context
Take quick turns

### Win-win problem-solving

Listen to both of your needs
Brainstorm options
Synthesize a proposal
Evaluate

*- from Thomas Gordon, Parent Effectiveness Training*

### Interrupting patterns of upset

Play with body habits
Reverse roles
Own responsibility
Forgive
Playfully claim the blame
Love the uglies

### The Glitch Process

1: Agree to do the Glitch Process.
2: Vent feelings without words.
3: Empathize with the other person's feelings.
4: Problem-solve together about the issue.
5: Appreciate each other and the process.

# Chapter 3
Grow through compassion

# Chapter 3: Grow through compassion

Many relationships sour because people want their partners to be different in some way, and they don't know how to support that to happen. They either criticize and nag at each other, or instead try to keep their negative thoughts to themselves. In either case, the result is not likely to be growth and harmony, but instead conflict or chilly distance.

This hefty chapter walks you through the skills of giving and receiving appreciation and empathy: two essential building blocks of loving, healthy, growing relationships. Once you and your partner gain proficiency in these delicious exchanges, you can apply those skills to respectfully help each other change, which is the focus of the final section of this chapter.

# Appreciation

We believe that most people are under-appreciated most of the time. The norm in society is to criticize and complain, rather than praise. In our culture, we rarely give explicit appreciation, and we're certainly not supposed to *ask* for appreciation. That's "fishing for compliments" and considered in very bad taste.

However, while this may be the norm in society at large, it doesn't have to be the norm in your relationship. Learning to exchange plentiful, genuine appreciation can give great pleasure as well as add to your bonding.

You or your partner may feel resistant at first to a structured appreciation process. You might feel that you don't deserve the appreciation... that it doesn't count if it's not spontaneous... that it's hard to let go of resentments... that the whole thing is embarrassing. To ease these feelings, at the start of each practice take a few minutes each to express whatever resistance you feel to giving or receiving appreciation, making sure to simply listen without response when the other partner is speaking. Then leap over these resistances and appreciate each other. Laughter or tears are fine.

## Practice abundantly

Set aside a specific time for you and your partner to practice appreciations. Even once a week for ten minutes can start to build the skill and habit. Once you feel warmed up to exchanging appreciations, integrate them abundantly into your daily life. Here are some of the many ways you can use appreciation to sweeten your life together:

### Notice everyday gifts

Every day, no matter how "basic" it is for one of you to take on a certain responsibility, take time to acknowledge each other's effort on your collective behalf. Regular appreciation and gratitude makes living together a treat.

> *"Thanks for doing the dishes, Crystal."*
> *"Thanks for cooking, James."*
> *"Thanks for making the bed, Pedro."*
> *"Thanks for changing that diaper, Yolanda."*

You may think, "This is silly, I shouldn't need thanks for what I do all the time." But even if you don't feel as if you *need* appreciation, you might be surprised at how good it feels to receive it. Accept the appreciation simply, by saying "You're welcome" or "Thanks for thanking me." No deflection (such as "I didn't do such a good job" or "It's no big deal") is allowed. The whole exchange takes about five seconds.

### Relieve tensions

Exchanging appreciations can be a powerful way to reduce resentments and to ease tension. You can use appreciations both as a ritual at the end of the day as well as when you notice distance between you. Practice directly offering it: "Is there anything you'd like appreciation for?" Practice directly asking to receive it: "Would you be willing to give me appreciation? Especially for…"

In any relationship, there are times when partners do unequal work. To reduce possible resentments, the partner doing less can acknowledge and appreciate the other person's contribution, framing the extra work as a gift to the relationship rather than a solitary burden.

> *Thanks for getting up in the night to nurse the baby, Sultana. I sure appreciate it.*

Appreciation is particularly soothing after working out a conflict, or in the middle of a difficult conversation when you both need a boost to keep going.

> *I'm feeling pretty raw from discussing this issue. Could we exchange appreciations for a few minutes before continuing?*

## Relish similarities and differences

Some people choose partnerships based on the comfort of similarities; others choose partnerships based on the stimulation of differences. Yet similarities can feel dull as well as sweet; differences can be grating as well as enlivening. Using the "even though" format below can acknowledge the challenge while giving the balm of specific appreciation.

> *Pauline, even though we cook together almost every day, I never take for granted how satisfying it is to enjoy same foods. (Appreciating a similarity)*

> *George, even though I like the freedom to be a little messy, I do appreciate how much you help us keep a tidy, serene, and beautiful home. (Appreciating a difference.)*

When appreciating differences, take care to offer appreciation without mixing in unmet needs or criticism.

## Reinforce the positive

A daily practice of exchanging appreciations can help you and your partner focus on and strengthen what is right in your lives, instead of letting you be preoccupied with what is wrong, missing or undone.

> *Michaela, what are 3 things you appreciate about:*
> *- how your life is on track?*
> *- our relationship?*
> *- what a good mother you are?*
> *- being alive in these interesting times?*

## Support personal growth

Many of us not only repeat to ourselves what is wrong with the world, but what is wrong with *ourselves*. We have rehearsed negative messages about ourselves for so long that we rarely even notice that we're doing it. It doesn't work to simply try and shut off the negativity recording. We need to replace them with new messages, ones that are vigorously practiced until they seem more real than the old self-put-downs. You can invite your partner to voice self-appreciation for ways they're trying to grow:

> *Anne, what are three things you appreciate about how well you take care of your stuff? (Asked by Christopher because he knows she's trying to be less absent-minded.)*

> *Christopher, what are three things you appreciate about how calm and relaxed you were this week? (Asked by Anne because she knows he's working to be less anxious.)*

If it is hard to see your own progress, it can sometimes help to put your self-appreciation in an "even though" format:

> *Even though I lost my temper with the kids yesterday, I do appreciate that there were three times this week I felt like yelling at them but didn't. I'm moving in the right direction.*

**Savor being together**

Cultivating a habit of daily appreciations can dispel taking each other's presence for granted. Appreciations help us wake up to how wondrous a gift our moments together actually are. Many couples do this in their first few months together, when they're still awed by the newness of being with each other. We encourage you to deliberately develop this as an ongoing practice, no matter how many years and decades you have been together.

Imagine how special you feel when, after coming home from a stressful day at work, your partner leaps up from his desk to hug you and says, "I'm so happy to see you! I love being partners with you!"

## Increase your appreciation skill

Have you ever had the experience of someone giving you an appreciation, but instead of feeling closer to the person you feel embarrassed or alienated? Or perhaps you've been the giver, and had the feeling that an appreciation you gave seemed to bounce off the recipient's surface, having no impact. How disappointing! Yet at other times, an appreciation can make your whole day, or touch your friend so deeply she weeps. What makes the difference?

There's an art to giving and receiving deeply nourishing appreciations. To make your appreciations more effective, work to embody qualities described below. Although these qualities are described from the giver's point of view, the recipient can also take the lead and request them. If you tend to be emotionally contained (because of sub-culture, family history, or personality) you may prefer to modify the tools in this section. Any appreciation is better than none! So don't let these more adventurous skills discourage you from giving simple appreciations in your own style.

## Connect

If you want your appreciation to hit home, make sure it's a good time for both of you to let it in. Take the time needed to connect to your heart and to fully express what you're feeling.

> *Basic appreciation: Thanks for coming home early to help me, Jolie (said while Jolie distracted putting away her coat).*
>
> *Connective appreciation: (Taking Jolie's hands and making eye contact) Jolie, it means a lot to me that you left work early today to help me with my work crunch.*

## Disclose what's meaningful to you

Sometimes appreciations fall flat when they are vague, positive judgments about the other person: "You're so beautiful," or "What a smart decision," or "I admire your bravery!" Being judged, even if positively, often falls short of providing the full nourishment that skillful appreciation provides. Instead, try to name very specifically the behavior or quality you're appreciating so the listener clearly pictures what you're referring to. Then take the time to describe vulnerably why it's meaningful to you.

> *Basic appreciation: Jolie, you are a life saver! My hero!*
>
> *Specific and self-disclosing appreciation: Jolie, I'm grateful you came home early to help me. I often feel alone with work. In my family growing up, any requests for help were seen as weakness. Your willingness to come help me feels healing as well as helpful.*

## Start with empathy

Beginning with empathy for your partner's feelings can help her let appreciation sink in, especially if she is stressed or distracted.

> *Basic appreciation: Wow, Jolie, I appreciate your coming home early to help me!*
>
> *Empathetic appreciation: Wow, Jolie, you left work early. I imagine that might have been hard, given how pressured you've been*

*lately. You coming home early to help me is especially meaningful to me since I know how much work you yourself have. Thank you!*

## Invite dialogue

Communication requires a "feedback loop" to feel complete. When you give an appreciation and then invite response, the conversation goes deeper.

*Request for feedback: Jolie, anything you want to say after hearing those appreciations?*

*Response: Well, you're right that I'm stressed at work, but that made it easy to leave. I wanted to get out of there. I forgot it's hard for you to ask for help, since it's easy for me. I'm glad my coming home means so much to you! I really didn't realize it.*

### Discover your partner's "love language"

We've focused here on the craft of giving and receiving verbal appreciations, but words are not the only, or necessarily the most important, way to express love. The book and website *The Five Love Languages* can help you to discern which modes of expression are most potent for you and your loved ones: words of affirmation, acts of service, receiving gifts, quality time, and physical touch. (And of course, there are far more ways to express love than these five.)

It can be eye opening to compare notes with your partner about which "love languages" hit home and which ones don't. Anne feels hugely loved when Christopher brings her a snack midday... and she doesn't care the least about gifts, not even on birthdays or anniversaries. Have you been expressing love through your words, when what your beloved needs to feel loved most may be a backrub? Once you've deciphered each other's preferred ways to feel loved, you can give each other what the other most craves.

# Empathy

## Understand what empathy is and isn't

We want our partners to understand our feelings. Being told: "you shouldn't feel that way," usually leaves us feeling angry and hurt, and with holding onto our feelings even more. Empathy, on the other hand, helps us let go of difficult feelings and move on.

We are often reluctant to empathize with each other because we confuse empathy with agreement. Empathizing simply means letting someone know you understand how he feels. It *does not* mean you support what he feels. It doesn't mean you agree with the reasons behind his feelings. Empathy means you can put yourself in his shoes and imagine accurately what is going on inside him, whether or not you agree.

## Regularly ask for and offer empathy

Like all the skills in this guide, empathy may feel awkward and artificial at first. (Notice that now we're empathizing with what you might be feeling in reading this.) It will become natural over time. Try it first when you're both calm. As you get more proficient, you can experiment applying the balm of empathy when you or the other person is upset.

### Ask for empathy:

> *Before you give your own viewpoint, it would really help me to know you've understood my feelings. Would you reflect back to me what I just said, especially the feeling part?*

### Offer empathy:

> *Would you like me to say what I understand, before I respond to what you just said?*

Empathy expressively reveals what you imagine your partner is experiencing. It is *not* just saying, "I understand how you feel" in a dutiful monotone. It sounds like: "I bet you felt frustrated being in that traffic jam, and probably anxious that I might be angry at you for being late!" or "Seems like you felt mad and hurt when I left without saying goodbye!" Make sure that your voice and manner genuinely expresses the emotion you're describing.

## Expect to try and try again

Sometimes when you try to empathize with your partner she may say (passionately) "No, that's not what I feel!" If you can respond without being defensive, you can keep the focus on your partner by saying simply, "What *do* you feel? I want to understand." Once she has expressed herself, try empathizing again to see if you've got it. "So you weren't angry; you were very frustrated. Not because I forgot the groceries, but because you were counting on baking something special for Louise's party." Perhaps this time she will say, "Yeah. Well. Sort of. You got the first part right, but you forgot to say..." Listen, and then try again. "Oh! You were frustrated because you wanted my *help* baking for Louise, and I came home too late to help you." "Yes, that's it!"

As with appreciation, any empathy is better than none, so don't hold back. But don't be too surprised if the first awkward attempts at empathy are inaccurate and so a little painful. To be empathized with fully and accurately feels as exquisite as getting a long cool drink when you're parched with thirst. Keep working at it until you make the connection.

## Mirror intense feelings

When your partner feels something intensely it can miss the mark to simply use words to empathize. Taking care to be sincere, join in with great expressiveness—perhaps even what may seem like exaggeration—to show you really get the full intensity of how it feels to your partner.

> *Weak joining: Janice, you must feel a bit disappointed to lose your mother's picture.*
>
> *Strong joining: Oh Janice, I mourn with you! I know how much that photo meant to you!*

You can also ask for more intense empathy.

> *Weak request for joining: I got the promotion! You can congratulate me.*
>
> *Strong request for joining: I got the promotion! Let's jump up and down and scream for a few minutes to celebrate!!!*

Sometimes it's enough to respond to invitations with a friendly nod or a murmur. But other times, our habitual ways of responding just won't do. Consider the following scene:

> *Elaine: I'd love us to plan a time to exchange massage this weekend. It's been too long.*
>
> *Jamie: Sure, that'd be nice. I'm not free this weekend, though.*

Responding in an extra expressive and empathetic way sometimes can make a big difference to your partner, especially when they have particularly strong feelings about something. Since vibrant responsiveness is rarely a daily habit, it takes practice. Either party can ask for a redo.

> *Jamie: Hmm ... Elaine, I see you look a little upset. Would you like me to give you a more responsive answer? OR*

> *Elaine: Hey Jamie, I felt vulnerable making that massage request. Are you actually interested? Would you be willing to make it clear to me if you are?*
>
> *Jamie: Sorry to give a distracted response! Yes, I'm interested, and yes, it has been a long time. I'm sorry I haven't had more attention for you. This weekend I'm flat out finishing that grant proposal, but I'd love to join you next Wednesday night. Does that work for you?*

Sometimes mild upsets can be put into perspective by exaggerated empathy. It's important that your partner understands what you're doing so she doesn't feel made fun of.

> *You were stuck in bad traffic for an hour?? How harrowing!!*

To us, the word "harrowing" describes extreme circumstances – like a brush with death. Using it playfully like this helps us gain perspective that bad traffic isn't actually a crisis while also empathizing with how much we hate it. We often ritually acknowledge each other's tensions with the phrase, "how harrowing!"

## Helping each other change

Here is a classic touchy situation, especially in a long-term relationship: You love your mate, but you wish she would change in certain ways, perhaps minor, perhaps major. "Be more ambitious." "Stop slouching." "Be less self-critical." "Learn to close the kitchen door without banging it." "Be on time."

You try to push aside your critical feelings, but eventually your annoyance leaks out. You try to talk it out, but your mate is quite defensive (even if she agrees with you, in theory). She doesn't change her behavior, and soon it's a sore point between you, a source of all-too-familiar arguments, hurt feelings, chilly avoidance, and even relationship break-ups.

Our relationship almost ended in year five when we were mired in these patterns. Anne thought if she could only criticize Christopher effectively enough—if he just understood how much pain she was in and how badly she needed him to change—then of course he'd be motivated enough to change. Instead, he felt defensive and abandoned with his difficulties.

Luckily we discovered that the key to helping your partner change is to keep clear about whose needs are being addressed. We dug ourselves out of our destructive criticism patterns by designing Positive Growth Campaigns, described below.

---

**Positive Growth Campaigns**

**Step 1:** Take time alone to each write two lists. First, what are some ways you want to change? Second, what are some ways you want your partner to change?

**Step 2:** Note where your lists overlap. See where a change you want for your partner is also a change he wants for himself. Select one area for each person to create a "positive growth campaign." See Step 4 for where your lists differ.

**Step 3:** The person aiming to change takes daily small steps and receives abundant appreciation for any moves in the desired direction, no matter how small. The person supporting the change acts as cheerleader and takes any frustrations elsewhere. See tips below.

> **Step 4:** Notice where your two lists differ: where you wish your partner would change but he doesn't care to, or where he wants a change in himself that you don't support. Discuss these items to discover if, after listening to each other, they become goals you share in common (or need acceptance of how you are now).
>
> Where your goals remain different, learn how to constructively handle your own reactions. It is valuable to let your partner know how and why her behavior affects you, and to get her thinking about how to meet your needs. But be clear this is a discussion about you, not about your partner.

### Tips for the person doing the changing

**Start small.** To achieve a change in behavior or personality, even a small one, usually takes consistent, long-term effort.

**Strengthen your resolve to change.** One way is to write down five reasons your life is hurt by the lack of change, five reasons why your life would benefit from the change, and five reasons why you believe you can change (such as people who can help you, strengths you have, past successes you can build on.) Read these lists frequently, and add to them.

**Break your goal into small steps.** As you take these steps expect to fall short again and again, especially if you're reaching for a substantial change. Forgive your mistakes and recommit to making the change.

**Bring friends into the campaign.** The more friends know what you're trying to do, the better. Coach them in positive reinforcement techniques, below. Take time with good friends to express and release whatever frustration, hopelessness, or other feelings that get in your way of taking action, so you don't need to only lean on your partner.

## Tips for the person supporting the other's change:

**Appreciate every little step in the right direction.** If possible, do this daily. Be a consistent, genuine cheerleader.

**Help your partner appreciate her own successes,** no matter how small. You can design question games that help her recognize the good ways she's changing. For instance, for someone learning to speak up for herself, you might ask, "What are three things you appreciate about how assertive you are?" or "What are three ways you spoke up for yourself this week?"

**Take negative feelings elsewhere.** Do not take them to your partner. If you have a backlog of frustrated feelings about your partner's lack of change—say, anger about how your own life is affected, fear that change will never happen, or wild impatience with her slow progress—express them in your journal, to a counselor, or to someone who doesn't personally know your partner. If you must vent to a friend who knows both of you, be sure to protect the relationships. "Could I have three minutes to complain about Ki? You know I love her and nothing I'm about to say is serious. I just need to release some frustration. Is that OK? Please hold what I'm saying in confidence."

**Stick with it.** Expect that the change will be longer and slower than you might wish. Forgive your partner's failures, help her recommit, and help her do problem solving that puts her in the driver seat. Remember, people are often unsuccessful in trying to change because they get frustrated and give up, especially if they're criticized by their loved ones instead of encouraged. Most people need massive doses of support and positive reinforcement to change. You can provide that.

## Grow through Compassion | 47

### Example when both partners want the same change

*Raiz' unconscious habit of chewing his lower lip drives Sophia crazy. She's especially embarrassed by it when they're in public. When they compared lists of things they wanted to change, she was pleased that this was something he wanted to change, too. He especially wanted to change the underlying cause of this habit: the chronic anxiety he carried in his body.*

*Together, Sophia and Raiz designed a positive personal growth campaign to address his anxiety and its symptoms such as lip chewing. He took up running and yoga and talked to his boss about some ongoing problems at work.*

*For the first month, they agreed that when in private, Sophia would make a sexy whistle if she saw Raiz chewing his lip, just to call it to his attention, but in public she'd do nothing. Also, at the end of each day Raiz would tell Sophia about three times he consciously did not chew his lip, so she could celebrate it with him.*

*In her journal, Sophia vented to herself about how often she still caught him chewing and how ugly it looked. After two months, Raiz was able to stop chewing his lip (mostly), but Sophia kept supporting him for another year on engaging in practices to address his anxiety.*

### Example when partners' goals differ

*Raiz wishes that Sophia would always be on time (or early) for events like he is. In fact, her frequent lateness, even when she's five minutes late, drives him crazy. He judges it as sloppiness and showing lack of respect.*

*Sophia, however, assesses herself as sufficiently punctual and does not particularly want to change this. So when they talk about this next it is Raiz' needs on the table, not hers.*

*Together they strategize about how to address his frustration: could he show up later? Bring a book? When they're meeting others, could he do a reality-check about whether they mind her minor lateness? Over time, Raiz becomes slightly more relaxed about punctuality and Sophia, no longer feeling judged, is more often right on time. But it continues to be an area of difference.*

To summarize, the key to helping your partner change is to keep clear about whose needs are being addressed. You do this by (a) finding out what your partner does and doesn't wants to change, (b) committing to offer the type of support she finds effective, and only that type of support, and (c) vulnerably asking for help with your own feelings.

## Healing the sources of pain

As therapists like to point out, our families of origin and our early life experiences greatly influence us, especially when it comes to how we cope in relationships. To get to the heart of conflicts, we often must delve into this more shadowy area, and do the personal work necessary to help ourselves (and our partners) heal from circumstances that have nothing to do with our current lives.

While many people choose to do healing work with skilled therapists, others choose to develop counseling skills to assist themselves, their friends, and their loved ones. We list a few resources for skill development at the end of this guide.

We hope that the example below, despite its brevity, will help illustrate what this healing might look like. Please note that the example is only offered for illustration, not to guide the inexperienced counselor.

We believe that healing early hurts is not only useful as "crisis" intervention, but as a valuable, perhaps necessary, component of supporting your relationship to be the best it can be.

## Explore early hurts

Vonda was extremely upset that her partner Jon "ignored her" the night before at a friend's party. After talking about it for an hour (using the "finding win-win solutions" process previously described) they figured out some ways to feel more connected at social events. Then their conversation continued...

> *Jon: I'm so glad we've talked about this! I feel good about our solutions.*
>
> *Vonda: Me, too. I'm very glad we eventually were able to listen to each other without being defensive.*
>
> *Jon: I'm still wondering whether what happened tonight at the party might have been connected to something from your past. What do you think?*
>
> *Vonda: (After thinking for a few minutes), You know, I didn't think of this before, but I'm remembering now how my father and my former husband acted at parties. Dad used to ignore my mom and flirt with other women, and Henry was always too caught up in "important" talks with other men to pay attention to me. Both of them made me feel worse than invisible. Just like I felt last night.*
>
> *Jon: Ow. I bet that was painful, having two important men in your life ignore you that way. I'm sorry if the way I acted last night stirred up old wounds. Would you like to explore this a little more with me?*
>
> *Vonda: Okay.*
>
> *Jon: Can you remember a time, years ago, when your father upset you at a party? Try pretending for a moment that you're back in that situation, and this time you have total permission to tell your father exactly how you feel and how you want him to treat you. Don't worry about what would be right to say to him in reality. Just express yourself as honestly as you can. You can even pretend I'm your dad, if you want, but I won't respond as he would. I'll just encourage you to express your feelings.*

*Vonda: I'll try. But remember I'm not saying this to you, Jon, just to my Dad, back when I was ten years old.... "Dad, how dare you treat Mom like that! How dare you flirt with other women in front of her! I'm so embarrassed! And how come you pay so little attention to me when we're with other people. Don't you dare say I'm such a cute little girl and then ignore me, you jerk!"*

*Jon: Yes, tell me more!*

*(Vonda yells more at her pretend father, and then yells and cries with her pretend past husband. Jon keeps encouraging her to express her feelings.)*

*Vonda: Whew! I'm exhausted! And amazed you could listen to me for so long! I feel lighter, and clearer. I didn't realize that so much of what was making me mad last night came from earlier in my life. Thank you so much!*

Re-evaluation co-counseling offers on-going classes, workshops, and publications to help lay people develop basic counseling skills. For many people, peer counseling is best supplemented by professional therapy.

## Commit to being allies

We not only have personal histories, but as social beings, we are very much affected by the conditions of the identity groups of which we are a part: male or female, gay or straight, Jewish or Gentile, etc. People are hurt in this society in many ways. Sometimes acknowledging larger societal patterns of oppression can help us, as individuals, realize that we are not personally responsible for some of the unconstructive behaviors we are caught in. Indeed, most of these behaviors and attitudes have been playing themselves out in the larger society long before we were born.

In addition to helping each other heal early personal hurts, partners can help each other heal by committing to being allies for each other across oppressed social identities (e.g. a man being an ally to a woman, or a white person being an ally to a person of color). Commit to being an ally to your partner even if you are not yet sure how to do it. You can learn how over time, both from your partner and from others who have worked to be allies across these differences.

> *Jon: You know, it seems to me what you experienced happens a lot between men and women. Men are taught to discount women, and women learn to feel powerless and invisible. I'm sorry for any ways that I may have learned to play into that hurtful male role. I want you to know that as a man I am committed to being your ally, to doing whatever I can to support you as a woman to be powerful. I hope you'll teach me how I can be an ally for you.*
>
> *Vonda: No man ever said such a thing to me before! I can't tell you how much it touches me, especially after seeing men treat women badly all my life. Thank you, Jon.*

Re-evaluation co-counseling (in the "Resources" section) is strong in explaining how societal oppression affects personal relationships, and offers support groups, workshops and journals specific to many identity groups.

## *Grow through compassion: key points*

### Use appreciation abundantly

- Notice everyday gifts
- Relieve tensions
- Relish similarities and differences
- Reinforce the positive
- Support personal growth
- Savor being together

### Appreciations go deeper when you:

- Connect to the recipient as you speak
- Describe specifics, not positive judgments
- Disclose what's meaningful to you
- Empathize with the recipient
- Invite dialogue

### Discover your partner's love language

- Words of affirmation
- Acts of service
- Receiving gifts
- Quality time
- Physical touch

*- From Gary Chapman, The Five Love Languages*

## Practice Empathy

Understand what empathy is and isn't
Regularly ask for and offer empathy
Expect to try and try again
Mirror strong feelings

## Help your partner change

Find out what your partner wants to change
Offer only the types of support she finds effective
Get help for your own feelings

## Design positive growth campaigns

**Step 1: Make two lists**
Ways you want to change
Ways you want your partner to change

**Step 2: Choose your campaigns**
Each choose one area where your lists overlap

**Step 3: Carry out positive growth campaigns**
Break your goal into small do-able steps
Lavish appreciation on every small step
Take frustrations elsewhere

**Step 4: Discuss where your lists differ**
See if any can become goals you hold together
If not, constructively handle your own reactions

### Tips when you're trying to change

Start small
Strengthen your resolve to change
Break your goal into small steps
Bring friends into the campaign

### Tips for supporting your partner to change

Appreciate every little step in the right direction
Help your partner appreciate her own successes
Take your negative feelings elsewhere
Know it takes time and persistence

### Healing the sources of pain

Explore early hurts
   -listen to each other
   -distinguish the past from the present
   -learn counseling skills and/or see therapists

Commit to being allies across power differences
   -pledge to interrupt oppressive behavior
   -support your partner's empowerment

# Chapter 4
Make decisions wisely

# Chapter 4:  Make decisions wisely

Couples make countless decisions together, some easy, but many tedious if not downright stressful. From the minor: "Shall we eat Italian or Chinese food tonight?" to the major: "Do we have kids together?" plus all the shades of importance in between: "Will we spend Easter with your family or Passover with mine?"  The need for decision-making relentlessly permeates our adult lives.

Making decisions with ease adds to the sweetness and the security of being partnered with someone.  In this section are some tools we developed after many struggles with less successful ways of making decisions together.  We now use these effective decision-making methods every day.

## Repetitive decisions

In ongoing relationships, certain decisions need to be made over and over, hundreds or thousands of times.  As couples get clearer about their needs and preferences, such decision-making can become quicker and easier.

One of the ways that couples handle repetitive decisions is to **alternate turns.**

> *We'll see your family during summer holidays and my family in winter holidays.*

Another way is to **create role divisions.**
> *You pay the house bills each month.  I'll handle our laundry.*

Another elegant short cut to repetitive decision-making we call **"rules of thumb."** These are useful in recurrent decisions where you want to choose freshly each time, yet where together you lack a clear preference or are ambivalent. Essentially, you agree in advance that the rule of thumb makes the decision for you. Then, if desired, you can still name any needs unmet by the decision and strategize how to meet them.

> *Shall we eat out tonight? Paulo has the slightest leaning towards eating out and Chris the slightest leaning to eat in. Their rule of thumb: "When in doubt, don't go out." They want eating out to remain special, not a habit, and to be conscious spenders.*
>
> *Chris: "Ok, since we have no clear combined preference, our rule of thumb is to eat in. Would you like to name what drew you to eat out?"*
>
> *Paulo: "I wanted some privacy from our housemates, plus I'm tired of cooking.*
>
> *Chris: "How about if I make dinner while you read alone. I'll bring it into our private work room and light a candle."*

You can deliberately use rules of thumb to nudge your relationship away from dulling habits and towards the direction of your deeper values. Here are idiosyncratic examples from our life:

> **Should we keep working or rest?** *Our rule of thumb: rest. It's so easy to be driven and keep working! Yet health is a strong value. Thanks to this rule of thumb, taking a 10-minute nap together has become a daily delight.*
>
> **Shall we get into water (swim, shower, walk in the rain) or stay dry? Rule of thumb: Get wet.** *We both feel instantly transformed by going in water, yet we're often resistant to each other's invitations. We're daunted by the hassle of changing clothes or by interrupting what we're doing. This rule of thumb inspires us to refresh ourselves more than we would otherwise.*
>
> **Shall we make love or do something else? Our rule of thumb: make love.** *Shifting into sexual energy sometimes sounds like more work than the satisfaction of handling our to-do lists or the relaxation of watching a movie. This rule of thumb helps us overcome reluctance and prioritize our sexual connection.*

*Shall we ask each other for help or do it ourselves? Our rule of thumb: ask for help.* When either of us feel burdened by the responsibilities of daily life, it can be hard to reach out. This rule of thumb reminds us not to assume the other is unavailable but instead as for the support we want.

# Tricky decisions

The following process for making decisions is the most thorough and useful one we've developed. At first glance, this process may seem cumbersome or complex. However, once you're fluent with the steps, it can be quick for most daily-life decisions and satisfyingly robust for the big ones. From the most minor decisions to the most difficult, following this can help your decision-making become straightforward, mutual, and even fun.

We call it the "Systematic Decision Making Process."

---

### Systematic decision-making process

**Step 1: Define the question.**
Articulate a simple choice between two options.

**Step 2: Name your leaning**
- Do you lean towards one of the options?
- If yes, is your leaning slight, medium or strong?
- If it's a joint decision, combine your leanings together.
- If desired, explain why you have that leaning.

**Step 3: Address concerns**
- When you imagine choosing the option you lean towards, what concerns come up for you?
- What are a few creative ways to address those concerns?
- If desired, you can invite a listener's opinions.

> **Step 4: Make your decision**
> - What is your leaning now?
> - Are you ready to make a decision?
> - If not, repeat steps 2 and 3 until ready to decide.
> - If yes, concisely summarize the decision made.
>
> **Step 5: Acknowledge lingering feelings**
> - Express any leftover feelings (e.g. regret, anxiety)
> - Do not confuse expressing feelings with changing your mind.

To give a simple illustration, here is Chico helping Alison make a decision about what to do tonight. His role is to ask her the questions and to keep the process moving briskly.

> *A: Would you help me make a quick decision?*
> *C: Sure! What's the question?*
> *A: Shall I go to the movies tonight or stay home?*

Make sure the question is clear and simple. Work on just one question at a time.

> *C: What leaning do you have, and how strong is it?*
> *A: I have a very slight leaning to go to the movies.*

Sometimes just calling this question cuts through a lot of ambivalence. It's fine for the person to say "no leaning" if she really has none. But don't let her sink into equivocating.

> *C: Why do you lean towards going?*
> *A: This is my one free night this week, and I really want to see the show playing down the street.*

Again, be sure the person sticks with why she has her leaning. Don't let her slip into why she's unsure. You may need to be assertive.

> C: Concerns to address?
> A: Yeah. When am I going to get that report written, if not tonight? And I'm worried I'll be tired tomorrow since the show ends at 11pm.

List all the concerns, without problem-solving yet.

> C: How could you meet those concerns? First, the report.
> A: Well, I could change my meeting with Janet to next week and work Thursday night instead. And if she can't switch, I could work late after the meeting. That would work.
> C: Good! How about your concern about being tired tomorrow?
> A: Tomorrow I could nap before dinner and go to bed early.

In this example, problem solving is straightforward, but often people need a lot of help to think up creative options and evaluate them.

> C: What's your leaning now? Ready to make a decision?
> A: Yes, I feel better about going. I'd like to call Janet about rescheduling our meeting, and then I'll ask Martha if she'll go with me to the nine o'clock show.
> C: Great. Regrets?
> A: I wish I had decided earlier so I could have made the seven o'clock show. And I wish you didn't have to work tonight so you could come with me!

## To make joint decisions

Each person states a leaning. Then these are combined into a collective leaning.

*Derek has a strong leaning for option A and Janice has a slight leaning for option A. Collectively they have a medium leaning for option A. They follow the process and both participate.*

Derek expresses a slight leaning for option B, while Janice names a slight leaning for option A. Collectively they thus have no leaning. They problem-solve together about both options, as described on the next page.

Derek has a slight leaning for option B but Janice has a strong leaning for option A, then collectively they have a slight leaning for option A. They then ask what concerns Derek would need to meet in order to go with the collective leaning?

Be aware of patterns in a relationship where one person typically states her preferences forcefully while the other understates his. In this case, you may need to compensate by weighing each person's expressed leaning differently, and in the long term, helping both be equally assertive.

### To make decisions when you have no leaning

If you truly have no leaning, then you can do problem solving quickly for both options. What concerns would you need to address in order to choose option A? What concerns would you address to meet in order to choose option B? Then check to see if a leaning has emerged. Usually one has.

### When you're ambivalent

If you use the process and still feel terribly ambivalent, then probably something more is needed. Perhaps clarity will come after expressing strong feelings or from figuring out how the decision stirs up personal issues from your past. Perhaps you need to meditate and ask a deeper part of yourself what you need. Then come back to the process and see whether you are clearer.

If fear is blocking you, it can help to frame the decision as between two fine options instead of between two bad (e.g., anxiety-provoking) options. Either one you choose is excellent! People who are burdened with habits of strong ambivalence can especially benefit from acknowledging that every decision comes with trade-offs and from using a clear process for decision-making.

# Weighty decisions

Sometimes in relationships we face decisions that are complex, have high stakes, and/or are highly charged emotionally. A few examples: to have children or not, to move or change careers, to end a pregnancy, to adopt a child, to break up or divorce, or to undergo a risky medical procedure. Many scary and difficult decisions are part of relationship life.

The Systematic Decision-making Process described above can still be valuable when wrestling with weighty decisions, so long as you add several additional steps. It helps to have practiced the process many times with less important decisions.

### Clarify the decision-maker(s)

Before Step 1, take extra care to clarify whether this is a joint decision, your decision, or your partner's. Think this through carefully. With many couple decisions, the decision must be made together. But some decisions need to be made or are better made by one person, even if the partner is strongly affected (for instance, whether to have a major medical procedure or choosing when to retire).

### Clarify the weight of each person's input

Even if it is a joint decision, one of you may have more input than the other. Even if you decide something is your final decision, you must still decide how much weight to give your partner's input.

### Vent emotional upset

If you're clogged with intense feelings, you won't be able to think clearly. Ask your partner or a friend you deeply trust (ideally, someone who is neither triggered by your decision nor directly affected by the outcome) to lovingly witness you for a specific amount of time while you express your feelings, such as grief, guilt, fear, and anger. Make it clear that his role is just to listen, not to fix the situation, offer opinions, or calm you down. Stick to your time agreement. Add this throughout the process as needed.

### Elicit useful advice

If you have decided that this is your decision (namely, that your partner may give input but is not a co-decision-maker), you might need to do extra work to be sure your partner's input is constructive. After Step 3 where you name and address concerns, ask your partner first to empathize with your feelings and summarize the interests you have named. Ask your partner to give advice that directly addresses those interests, before your partner names and addresses his own values and interests. (If this is an emotionally challenging decision for the partner, he may need to get additional support elsewhere or even need to bow out of playing this tender role.)

### Give yourself time to sit with the decision

When you feel close to having made the decision, name a time frame to try on your decision before finalizing it. You might want to sit with it for hours, days, even weeks or months.

### Practice communicating your decision

If you are making a decision you expect will be painful to your partner, practice how to be clean and clear about what you decided and why. Clearly communicate what you need to say to your partner.

To illustrate these additional steps of a weighty decision, we'll follow Yvette who has learned she has a late-stage cancer and is making the very difficult decision about how to respond.

>  **Vent strong feelings:** Yvette asks her husband, Olivier, if he is open to listening to her grief, terror, and rage about having cancer. She also asks her women's group to give her space for these feelings and finds a therapist, so it is (hopefully) less of an emotional burden for Olivier.
>
> **Clarify the decision-maker:** Yvette determines that she will make the decision herself about treatment, not have it be a joint decision with her husband. She gets input from her doctor and is also clear that it is not the doctor's decision.
>
> **Clarify the weight of each person's input.** Yvette tells Olivier she will consider very seriously his feelings and thoughts, but at the end of the process, requests that he honor her wishes and let go of trying to influence her further.
>
> **Elicit useful advice.** Yvette asks Olivier to tell her what he understood of her feelings, core values and hopes, after he has listened awhile. Yvette asks him to then give advice that is based on those understandings as fully as he can. Then she asks him to state his feelings, values, and hopes and to offer his own input.
>
> **Give yourself time to sit with the decision.** After a month of research, weighing options and getting her loved one's input, Yvette makes a tentative decision but still feels terrified. So she decides to give herself another 48 hours to sit with that leaning and pray about it before finalizing the decision.
>
> **Practice communicating the decision.** Yvette role-plays in her women's group telling Olivier that she has decided (against her doctor's advice) that for the next 3 months she will only do alternative treatments. She requests that he share his fear and grief with her, but then take those feelings to other friends for support. Yvette requests Olivier join her for a 15-minute daily prayer time for both of them.

Decisions as complex and emotionally charged as these can be extremely challenging even with the best tool kit. By practicing the systematic decision-making process for your daily decisions, you can become skillful enough to lean on it for the whammy decisions life brings.

## Agreement-check

Whenever you've made a decision together, whether major or minor, take a few moments to be sure you're actually on the same page. Couples often feel frustrated when one person thought the other had agreed to something, yet the other remembered it differently or didn't even think it was a decision.

> *Sorry, I thought 10am was just a rough time for us to start work together. I didn't think it mattered if I arrived 15 minutes later.*
>
> *You wanted to be the one to call your mom? I thought we said whoever could get to it first was fine.*
>
> *You thought I was going to buy the plane tickets? I thought you were going to!*

This glitch may not be a problem of poor memory, but rather of not taking the time to carefully check that a) you both are consciously making an agreement, and b) you are agreeing to the same thing.

We designed the following ritual as a way to be sure we're on the same page.

## Ritual to check agreements

Step 1: Confirm you're both ready to make an agreement.
Step 2: Summarize it.
Step 3: Verbally check for agreement.
Step 4: Signal physically to affirm the agreement.

> *Angel: Seems like we're ready to decide to go away for the weekend? Is that right?*
>
> *Murielle: Yes! We've agreed to drive off on Friday between 7 and 7:30pm and get home sometime (to be decided later) Sunday afternoon. Is that's what we're deciding?*
>
> *Both: Yes!*
> *Both: High five!! (They clap hands)*

# *Make decisions wisely: key points*

### Streamlined repetitive decisions

Alternate turns
Create role divisions
Make "rules of thumb"

### The Systematic Decision-Making Process

Step 1: Define the question between two choices
Step 2: Name your leaning
Step 3: Address concerns
Step 4: Make your decision
Step 5: Acknowledge lingering feelings

### For weighty decisions

Add these steps to the Systematic Decision-Making:
Vent emotional upset
Clarify the decision-maker(s)
Decide the weight of each person's input
Elicit useful advice
Give yourself time to sit with the decision
Practice communicating the decision

**Ritual to check agreements**

Confirm you're both ready to make an agreement
Summarize what has been agreed upon
Check for agreement and affirm with a physical gesture

# Chapter 5
## Hot topics

# Chapter 5: Hot topics

When we wrote the first version of this guide, we were overwhelmed as new parents to our son, and still raw from the stillbirth of our daughter the previous year. We had barely begun our careers and were less familiar with the stresses that work brings to relationship. The challenges of middle age weren't even on our minds.

Now that we're pushing 60, we have updated this guide with some of what we've learned and invented in the intervening years, especially ideas and tools related to the "hot topics" that follow. As we mentioned in the introduction, we're not trying to be comprehensive about any of these five topics. There are many books and training programs in each of these areas that go into much greater depth. We're only seeking to share a little of what's been helpful to us, imagining that some of it might also be helpful to you.

## Sexuality

For many couples, sex is easy and exciting at the start of their relationship, but as life pressures increase, and as years and decades go by, sex may become increasingly stale, sparse, or even non-existent. Although our culture is more open than it used to be around sexuality, it is still private and vulnerable territory for many of us, with few opportunities for exchange or guidance. Many have a relationship to sexuality that is unhealthy or worse: inhibited, compulsive, and sometimes even abusive. We make no claim to have great expertise in this area, but we have worked on it. Below are some of the practices and resources that are making a difference for us currently, as we explore how to savor greater sexual connectedness even as our sexual energy wanes.

## Make sexual dates

Many of us acquired the misconception (perhaps from seeing movies where ecstatic couples tear off each other's clothes) that in order to be genuine, lovemaking should just happen spontaneously as we feel swept up in desire. But for many couples over 40, for those exhausted from kids and/or demanding jobs, or for those who have been together a long time, that type of desire may happen rarely. If you rely on spontaneous combustion, being sexual together is likely to be less and less frequent. Making sexual dates keeps sex in your life.

At first, planning a specific time for sex may seem unbearably contrived. You might think, "If my partner needs to schedule time for sex, then he doesn't really desire me!" Or it may seem like pressure: "I can't get aroused on demand!" Or too vulnerable to suggest: "What if I'm now refused—again!" The sections below address some of these concerns.

### Say yes...and then negotiate

Here's our rule: all invitations for sex dates are answered with a "yes," although the time can be negotiated. This rule provides active encouragement for invitations and removes the fear of rejection.

### Decide what type of date

A sexual date is simply an invitation to give and receive intimate pleasure. Within that broad definition many kinds of connection are possible. Talk together about what kind of date you'll have, either when you're scheduling the date or when your date starts.

If you feel awkward or embarrassed talking about sex (as many do), deciding what kind of sexual date to have offers great practice to be better able to discern and articulate what you truly want. Here are some possibilities to get you started, taken from the books *Hot Monogamy* and *Expanded Orgasm* listed in the Resources section.

> ***Sensual:*** *Deliberately keep genital touching and orgasm off limits. You can still get aroused, but the focus is on giving and receiving sensual pleasure.*
>
> ***The usual:*** *Make love in whatever ways are most comfortable and easy for you both, without needing to be creative or cial. Relax and enjoy.*
>
> ***Leisurely:*** *Set aside twice or three times as much time as you usually take for lovemaking. What you do might not be much different, but the feeling will be more spacious.*
>
> ***Quickie:*** *You may sometimes enjoy something short and sweet when the energy is there, or just necessarily brief due to lack of more time. Sometimes you might decide to offer one-way attention to the person who gets most easily aroused or the one who most craves the attention at that time.*
>
> ***Adventurous:*** *Select together something you rarely or never do, and give it a try. See the book Hot Monogamy for a list of possibilities.*
>
> ***Purposeful****: Experiment with exercises to help you overcome stuck or awkward places in your sexual connection. During "sexercises," partners often give and receive feedback more intentionally than in usual love-making. Sexercises take work (although the work can be fun). The books in the resource section offer many sexual exercises. See also "Feedback" section below.*

### Take time to transition

Artists and athletes know that warm-ups are essential to performance. For instance, a singer might take 30 minutes to stretch her body and do gentle vocal scales before singing.

Good lovemaking comes from being in your body, present in the moment, emotionally open, and connected to your partner. It's a far cry from how many of us spend our days: sitting at the computer or doing other body-stressing activities, rushing through lists of things to do, feeling pressured, and disregarding our feelings.

Figure out what helps each of you transition into a state conducive to lovemaking. Your ways of transitioning could be quite different for each of you. If you're having a pre-planned sex date, decide whether to include transition time in your sex dates, or agree that you'll each take transition time before your date starts. Consider these components:

> **Body:** What helps you connect to your body in a good way? A hot shower... stretching... mild exercise... massage... a nap... Avoid your e-mail!
>
> **Mind:** What helps you let go of past or upcoming tions? Talking about them... writing a list for later... handling one last thing... prayer... meditation...
>
> **Emotion:** What does your heart need to feel peaceful and connected? Journal-writing... listening... emotional release through tears or laughter...
>
> **Environment:** What's important to you? Candles...beauty... music... comfort... privacy...

## Give and receive feedback

The idea that we should psychically "just know" how to please our partner is a damaging myth. While some couples do have powerful sexual attraction or "good chemistry," other couples don't. Even when couples enjoy great sexual chemistry, sex is a set of skills that improve with practice. Yet, while making love, many shy away from giving and receiving feedback, feeling awkward or simply fearing to interrupt the flow. We recommend finding low-stress times to talk about sex, and developing a toolkit of exercises to help facilitate connection and communication.

### Agree on a feedback time

Decide on a particular date ahead of time to experiment with giving and receiving feedback. The goal here is simply to improve your communication or to work on some edge for either of you, not fabulous lovemaking per se.

### Remember that every moment is fresh

For many people, especially women, what they find arousing changes from moment to moment. What "works" one time won't necessarily work the next. So the goal is not to memorize rules or patterns of what's arousing, but rather to become adept at reading your partner's subtle (or not so subtle) cues, and to become relaxed at giving and receiving feedback in the moment.

### Mix appreciation and encouragement with requests

Notice and tell your partner when something feels good. "Mmm, I like your tongue there!" Then make one very specific simple request in a relaxed voice. "Lighter." Then affirm that change before making another one "Mmmm, better! Could you do the same thing even lighter?" That makes two appreciations for every request.

For more feedback ideas see the books *Expanded Orgasm* and *The ESO Program*, in the Resources section at the end.

### Find language you both like

Much of the language for sexual acts and body parts can sound either crass or clinical. Play around together and choose or create words you both enjoy.

We've made up names for four kinds of touch: "earth touches" (firm massage or compression), "water touches" (smooth and flowing), "air touches" (light and tingling), "fire touches" (with intent to arouse). What new language might be helpful to you and your partner?

**Make up simple exercises or games**
Some people find it hard to know or describe what feels good or what they want. Creating games that offer very simple choices can make this more fun and easy. Here are some simple games that we came up with:

Variation game
Partner A is arousing Partner B in a specific way. Partner A then asks: "Which of these three variations do you like better? Here's #1… now #2…. now #3….."

Partner A tries to make each variation distinct and to do each for at least a minute. (Of course, B might be getting increasingly aroused through the sequence, so it's not exactly a scientific test!) Partner A might even put into words exactly what A's doing each time before she does it, so B can better picture what A is doing.

B aims to relax and enjoy. B feels free to say, "Do that one again" or "Move on to the next one." After B has experienced all three, B tries to describe not only which B preferred but why. Remember that this is just a preference of the moment, not for all time.

Options game
Partner C verbally offers three distinctly different lovemaking activities that involve arousing Partner D: "Would you rather I do this… or this… or this?" They must all be things that genuinely appeal to C to do.

D then chooses one and C does it. If C requests it, D can try to explain why, or say his response to each of the offers. (D: "They all appeal, but I think I'd need to be more aroused before experiencing #1 and #3.)

Then switch roles.

Theme game
Together they choose a theme. The theme provides a focus or limit for each partner during this time of lovemaking. Then they talk afterwards about what each enjoyed (or didn't enjoy) about that theme. Some examples of themes:

- One of you keeps eyes closed the whole time.
- Maintain much more (or much less) eye contact than usual.
- Kiss much more (or much less) than you usually do.
- One of you is dressed and the other naked.

**Try OM-ing**
"OM" stands for Orgasmic Meditation, a specific practice of giving 15-minutes of one-way, genital touching, usually to a woman, a term coined by Nicole Daedone written in her book Slow Sex. This deceptively simple practice has been powerful for many couples, in part because it creates a safe practice that even very busy people can invest in, one where the recipient can release performance anxiety and relax into receiving sexual attention. It often untangles the mystery, embarrassment, and confusion that can surround female arousal, and partners learn a great deal about giving and receiving feedback.

## Work with yin and yang energies

Traditional Chinese Taoist philosophy speaks of the complementary duality of yin and yang, both essential for wholeness. Yin is associated with softness, yielding, the moon, nighttime, and femininity. Yang is associated with hardness, forcefulness, the sun, daytime, and masculinity.

The difference between yin and yang energies can supply dynamic energy to sexual connection. Every person has yang ("masculine") energy and traits, as well as yin ("feminine") traits in different proportions. It helps to know and accept which type of energy is more natural to each partner and which is a turn-on. In both heterosexual and in same-sex relationships, couples can be fed by expanding and savoring these differences rather than by reducing or denying them.

In the past generation, as a result of the feminist, gay rights, and queer movements, gender roles have become less rigid. Much of that has helped create healthier relationships between men and women (e.g. it has helped men be more receptive and women more powerful, and increased both women and men's sense of wholeness). However, feminist men sometimes confuse the wonderful commitment to be non-sexist with unnecessarily holding back (or letting atrophy) their potent, sexy yang energy. Feminist women sometimes confuse being powerful with unnecessarily denying their receptive, sexy yin energy.

Sex writer David Deida's controversial books speak eloquently to the interplay of yin and yang. Yin partners can be like the ocean, buffeted by ever-changing emotions. They want their passionate, fluid feelings to be welcomed in a non-reactive way. At the same time, they long to be held steady by the strong directionality of their yang partners, to be "penetrated by their love" both literally and physically.

Often, yin partners need to feel emotionally close before they can open up sexually, while yang partners need sexual connection first in order to open up emotionally. This difference alone has caused many couples to stalemate. Instead, partners can begin lovemaking by taking turns giving each other attention for 5-10 minutes. The yin partner can first receive cuddling and empathetic listening... perhaps a chance to cry... then the yang partner can receive whatever sexual attention the yin partner now feels ready to give. After full lovemaking the yang partner might be more receptive to receiving emotional attention.

### Expect difficult emotions

Many people have experienced some form of sexual abuse and need years of personal growth and/or therapy to heal from that legacy. But even for people with no traumatic history, difficult feelings can arise during lovemaking: fear, sorrow, shame, loneliness, guilt, or anger... feelings that may be completely unrelated to the present moment or relationship. Learn how to help each other safely explore and release those feelings without taking them personally. Below are just a few of the many sexual topics where irrational feelings are bound to arise. See also "Healing the sources of pain" section earlier in this guide.

### Feelings about different desire levels

Many of us have a history of feeling either pressured to have sex or rejected for wanting sex (or both) and we can easily fall into our familiar pattern. For the partner who wants less sex, feeling pressured or obligated can erase genuine desire; for the one who wants more, feeling needy or rejected can generate resentment and withdrawal. This can be great territory for playing with the "role reversals" described earlier in this guide. For instance, if your partner has a history of being rejected for wanting sex, set up a role reversal where you ask your partner to make love, who vociferously refuses you again and again. You might both laugh a lot.

### Feelings about different turn-ons

If one of you feels uncomfortable with a proposed sexual activity, instead of assuming that territory is off limits, can you welcome the feelings? Set aside time separate from lovemaking to explore them. Take turns as speaker and listener. Encourage the person to express and even exaggerate their negative reactions (e.g., "Yuck! Gross! I would NEVER do that!"). Listener, take nothing personally! Explore the roots of both desire and repulsion. After some tears or laughter, you might be able to more easily find some common ground.

### Feelings about aging

Sexual energy often declines with aging and brings new relationship challenges. We address this in the "Aging" section.

### Feelings about fertility

Especially for people who have had childbearing issues (such as trouble conceiving, abortions, miscarriages or stillbirths, or more or fewer children than they wish for) having sex can bring unbidden emotions, even years and decades later. Don't be surprised. Allow room for the feelings.

A related aside: For the two of us, "Fertility Awareness" was a wonderful way to both prevent and assist conception. It was our primary form of birth control for three decades. We highly recommend it for couples who communicate well and have the discipline to adhere conscientiously 100% to the key principles. See resource section for more information.

## Make agreements about exclusiveness

Most of us were raised with the assumption that monogamy is the right and only way to show committed love. Many consider adultery a sin. Even for those who don't have religious views on this, many believe that if someone in the couple "cheats" and the "ugly truth" comes out, that's likely the end of the relationship.

OK, here we have views that may be troublesome to some readers. We respect that people have different values. Personally, however, we are pained to witness how the strict and emotionally volatile belief that monogamy is the only option for stable relationships has brought suffering to incalculable numbers of people. Pure monogamy works beautifully for some couples. But evidently it does not for a great many others, including many couples that espouse it.

Exclusiveness means different things for different people. For example, for some people just thinking sexual thoughts or being close friends with another person other than your partner is threatening. Others have more relaxed boundaries, and many aren't sure what their boundaries are until they get crossed. As with everything in this guide, our bias is towards partners practicing honest communication. Through skillful and compassionate listening to get at each partner's underlying needs, you can creatively negotiate agreements rather than assume hard and fast rules.

This kind of openness is very different from the secret intimacies many couples maintain. Even though hidden relationships sometimes "work" (e.g. we know one loving marriage that survived for 50 years in part because one partner had a long-term "secret" lover), for us, keeping secrets is a violation of the trust that underlies deep closeness. We endorse openness and trust, not secrecy.

Even in sub-cultures where people are open to exploring non-monogamous arrangements, pulling off respectful "open relationships" is a considerable feat. As a practice it demands an extraordinary level of personal self-awareness, communication skill, sensitivity to others, and willingness to process what comes up for everyone. We're humbled by how much work open non-monogamy takes to do well, as we both experienced in our early 20s and have seen over the years from friends who are committed to open or poly-amorous relationships.

Below are two different real-life examples of people happy in unconventional and non-exclusive relationships. The names have been changed to protect privacy.

> *Izzy and Jules have been happily married and mostly monogamous for 30 years. There is one exception: once or twice a year, Izzy spends the weekend with a lover, a woman he was involved with before he met Jules. Despite some awkwardness about it in the early years of their marriage, this has been a remarkably stress-free arrangement. The woman, too, is in a solid marriage with good communication, and her husband is similarly unthreatened by this sexual connection. The energy between the lovers primarily is one of friendship, not an ongoing romantic preoccupation that could easily stir jealousy.*
>
> *Tiffany and Beth savored ten years of a devoted monogamous relationship. Then, over the next ten years, they gradually added Paula to their lives as a second sexual partner for Tiffany and as*

*a close friend for Beth. All three now co-parent the children and are accepted as a committed threesome by their in-laws. (In their professional lives they are "out" about being gay but not "out" about their non-monogamy.) To achieve this stable, happy and unconventional state has taken hundreds of hours of skillful processing and careful agreement setting. Because all three of them view polyamory as part of their life's work as agents of cultural change, they do not resent the investment it has required.*

If you are drawn to venture into open, non-monogamous territory—even to nonsexual, intimate relationships that could be threatening to your partner—here are a few of our suggestions:

**Attend first to your primary relationship.** Make sure you are not using other relationships as an "easy" way to get around areas of discontent in your primary relationship. Deal with those first and foremost.

**Talk about non-sexual closeness.** Discuss with your partner how you both feel about nonsexual yet intimate relationships with other friends. Consider different types of situations, as well as how you feel about closeness to people of each gender. For example, how do you each feel about: friendly snuggling, intense dancing, frequent texting, long phone conversations, trips that include overnight stays…. when the primary partner is present… or absent? Know that predicting reactions in theory may be quite different from what happens in reality.

**Listen in turns.** Be sure to leave plenty of room for each of you to express your feelings. Take turns listening. Listen some more. Explore what needs (e.g., for security, trust, communication, adventure, companionship) underlie the feelings and discuss creative ways to meet important needs, either within the relationship, or with others, as you are both comfortable.

**Expect many conversations.** Expect to have these conversations many times, as needs, feelings, and situations change.

**Be discreet.** If you choose to be sexually non-monogamous, be thoughtful about discussing your choices with others. Most people have strong beliefs and feelings about this and passionately disapprove of (or feel threatened by) alternative arrangements. Don't expect all your friends and family to support your experiments.

**Find allies.** On the other hand, do find support. Others have walked the road of open relationships and you can learn from friends, local support groups, books, or online research.

**Keep agreements.** Above all, negotiate clear agreements. Scrupulously uphold all decisions you make together in order to maintain each other's trust, and evaluate and revise these agreements as often as needed.

## *Sexuality: key points*

**Make sexual dates**

Say yes…then negotiate when and what
Decide what type of date

**Take time to transition**

Decide if transition time is solo or together
Attend to body, mind, emotion, and environment

**Give and receive feedback**

Agree on a feedback time
Remember that every moment is fresh
Mix requests with encouragement
Find language you both like
Make up simple exercises or games
Try OM-ing

## Work with yin and yang energies

Celebrate and play with the differences
    Men can be strongly yang and still non-sexist
    Women can be deeply yin and still empowered

Creatively address the needs of both energies
    Yin opens to sex after emotional closeness
    Yang opens to emotional closeness after sex

## Expect difficult feelings

Old feelings often arise in sex about issues like
- desire levels
- turn-ons and turn-offs
- aging
- fertility

Don't take feelings personally. Take turns. Empathize.

## Make agreements about exclusivity

Attend first to your primary relationship
Discuss non-sexual closeness
Listen in turns
Expect many conversations
Be discreet
Find allies
Keep agreements

# Money

According to a report on CNBC, 90% of marriage break ups are because of money. Need we say more?

The two of us have been incredibly lucky to have ample financial slack throughout our years together. So we can't speak personally to the lack-of-money stress that wracks (and wrecks) many couples. Nonetheless, it's taken work to blend our different money backgrounds, values, and styles. All the skills described earlier—taking turns, empathizing, being clear whose needs are on the table—have made a huge difference when tackling this touchy subject.

You can find thousands of helpful books and websites about money management in general; below are just a few of the specific money-related concepts and tools that helped us as a couple.

By the way: our profession for 30 years was promoting conversations about money and values. See *More than Money Journal* in the resource section to access a treasure trove of 43 free back issues of money stories and wisdom.

## Exchange money histories

For many people, money carries a complex and emotionally charged history. It can feel vulnerable simply to talk about money, much less to actually share finances. Money easily brings up feelings of power and powerlessness, of judgment and fear of judgment.

Early in a serious relationship, before starting to share money, we recommend taking time to tell each other your money histories. Since there's often so much to tell, you might do it over several sessions, with each of you sharing on a particular topic (e.g., your parents' and grandparents' financial and class situations... positive and negative money messages from your family of origin... how you related to money as a child, as a teenager, and as a young adult... your work history... areas of financial competence and incompetence, where you feel pride and shame, confusion and clarity... how you handled money in previous relationships... your experiences and values in earning, spending, saving, and giving...). If the conversation becomes emotionally intense, take short turns, rotating between talking and listening to your partner. Be sure to empathize with your partner's feelings before asking questions or tackling differences. By taking the time for these conversations, you'll be in much better shape to join your financial futures, as you'll both be more aware of each other's strengths and challenges.

Building on what you've learned from exchanging money histories, each person try to name both the strengths and limitations of your own money style. Then discuss how each person's distinct strengths might serve your collective financial lives, and how you might use each other to shore up your individual weaknesses.

> *Preston's nuclear family struggled for basic necessities, while Derrick grew up with relative abundance. Not surprisingly, they developed very different money styles. Over time, they learned to appreciate that Preston's experience led him to be a thorough and careful money-manager, something that has greatly benefitted the couple's joint life. He has helped Derrick understand key financial concepts and make more thoughtful choices. And Derrick's more relaxed attitude about money has helped Preston enjoy the money they share without habitual anxiety.*

## Address differences in power

This article of ours and cartoon by Johnny Lapham are adapted from "Balance of Power," in *More than Money Journal*, issue #5.

Many couples strive for a sense of equality and balance in their intimate relationships. They hunger for partnerships where both people feel powerful: able to get what they want in the relationship and in their own lives.

Large money differences often upset this dream of equality. The one with greater income or assets in a couple is frequently perceived by both parties as having more power: more influence over the couple's decisions, more freedom to craft his or her own life, and more authority to decide whether and how the couple will share financial resources.

In other areas of life, the rules of social interaction usually cushion people from confronting economic differences directly. For example, people may work side-by-side with others earning twenty times more or less than they do, but they don't ask their co-workers, "How do you feel about our difference in pay?" Couples who cross social or economic strata in their intimate relationships cannot avoid these painful questions. They are challenged to meet economic differences head on, opening their hearts as well as minds.

For many people, financial differences and power imbalances are hard to untangle because they are so emotionally charged. Here are a few of the complex feelings people struggle with:

For those with less money:

> *I'm embarrassed to even bring up the subject of money. I'd hate for her to think I'm greedy or out for her money. Besides, it's hers.*

> *I resent having to be the one to bring this up. If Howard trusted me, he would just treat the money as ours.*

> *I'm scared to assume responsibility for Fred's money. He grew up learning to manage it, and I was taught nothing about it.*

For those with more money:

> *I feel ashamed that I've barely taken control of my money. I'm afraid if I share my money with Peter he'll be just like my dad, either mocking me or taking over.*

> *I'm scared to share money with Joan because I'm not convinced she's completely committed to us being together. But the problem is circular: it seems her discomfort with our money differences makes it hard for her to commit.*
>
> *I feel critical of how Jonathan uses money, and so don't want to share what I have. I don't know what to do about my judgments.*

Some couples try to tiptoe around their power differences, fearing that talking about them will open a "Pandora's Box" of unsolvable issues. But differences left unaddressed often deepen into chilly reservoirs of distance and mistrust. On the other hand, with persistent work (done gently and respectfully), even complicated and emotionally charged imbalances can be untangled and resolved over time.

If you and your partner are trying to reduce your money-related power differences, you might find yourself working through the following steps:

**Step 1: Voice discontents.** Most often, one of you will start to voice (sometimes indirectly) frustration with the power dynamics in the relationship. Soon both of you are unhappy with the economic arrangements. Even if neither of you feel ready yet to change your arrangements or know what to do yet, this uncomfortable stage is actually an important first step towards greater balance.

**Step 2: Recognize societal influences.** Part of the healing process is to notice how the relationship is influenced by dynamics from the wider society. Your challenges are not just personal! Financial differences are often complicated by experiences of societal discrimination (or privilege) due to gender, race, class, age, disability, religion, etc. For instance, compared to a partner from a "dominant" group (e.g., male, white, upper-class) a partner from a "subordinate" group is likely to have less earning power, less credibility competing for higher status jobs, and less self-confidence about his or her power in the world. It's important to unpack the societal as well as family baggage so people can be sensitive to what's likely to be potentially painful or even traumatic to the other, and to explore how to be helpful.

These social differences may exacerbate financial inequalities (for instance, when an upper-class white person is building a relationship with a working-class person of color) or create confusing crosscurrents (for instance, when someone who is wealthy and young is with someone who is older and working-class).

**Step 3: Dialogue.** Take the time and establish the trust to talk directly about how you each experience the money and power differences in the relationship. Use the skills described earlier in this guide: taking turns, empathizing, knowing whose needs are on the table. Explore the effects of dominant and subordinate roles on your relationship to money. Seek support of others from your own background to grow in awareness and heal from the past.

Ask each other what has been good and what has been hard about being from your own class backgrounds, and listen deeply to each other's stories. Affirm your commitment to be together and validate the important qualities you each bring, despite your differences, to the relationship and to your lives.

**Step 4: Explore options.** Once both of you feel that your differing life histories have been heard and respected, you can more constructively discuss the nitty-gritty of what you want financially. Don't hesitate to get technical and emotional support from friends and financial professionals. Aim to generate a range of possible options that could move your financial relationship in directions you want to go.

**Step 5: Experiment and evaluate.** Choose among the various options and come up with creative ways to move towards balancing financial power in manageable steps. (See "Four aspects of financial sharing" below.) After a designated time of implementation, discuss how well your experiments are meeting your goals and revise them as needed.

## Decide what to share

Many people assume that if they've "become a couple" they should share money 100%, and if they don't, there must be something wrong with the relationship. In reality, there are endless creative, compatible ways in which couples can both share and keep separate their financial lives.

We've found it helpful to name four different aspects of financial sharing, to discuss each of them separately, and to know that any arrangements made can shift over time. In none of these four areas does sharing need to be "all or nothing."

**Sharing expenses:** This is usually the first area to arise, as couples figure out who pays for what and why. Negotiations sometimes start on the first date. There's no rule that says couples must split shared expenses 50-50, or must split all types of expenses the same. All sorts of variations can work as long as agreements are mutual, clear, followed, and regularly evaluated as needs change.

**Sharing day-to-day management:** Whoever takes on more of the daily money management (i.e. paying the bills, handling banking and investing, writing checks to charity, taking care of taxes, etc.) often experiences greater financial clarity and influence. If most or all daily money management is handled by one partner, you can help balance the power by having regular check-ins, perhaps every 2-4 months, to be sure the less-involved partner fully understands what's being done and why.

**Sharing decision-making:** Decision-making about money can be separate from legal ownership. For instance, you could pool your savings into one account to put into investments, but decide that one partner will be making all the investment decisions. Or you could decide to make charitable decisions together, even though the accounts you each donate from are legally separate and you have different amounts of money in them.

Even if you keep your day-to-day financial decision-making separate, your life together is hugely affected by the values that guide your long-term money decisions. What ultimately is the money for? How much do you need to feel secure? If you have or anticipate financial surplus, how will you decide what to do with it? These big decisions can be shared or not. Even if a pre-nuptial agreement keeps your assets legally separate, you can choose to give each other decision-making influence over actions related to your money—or not.

**Sharing ownership**: If you have sufficient trust between you, you might legally transfer money to joint ownership, whether or not you are legally married. Sharing financial ownership can happen quickly, over time, or not at all. Even if you never share ownership over your money, you can still share expenses, decision-making and/or money management.

### Make written plans together

How do you know if you're on the same page about money? Few things have helped us as much as creating written plans together: spending plans, a lifetime financial plan, a multi-year giving plan, and an estate plan or will. Even though the pressures of daily life make it difficult to carve out time for these important but not-urgent plans, the returns can be enormous: greater peace of mind and ability work out differences.

We believe that the clarity these plans can give you over the long haul as a couple will make them well worth their time and effort. You can spread the work out over time – for instance, have a goal of making one type of plan per year for the next four years.

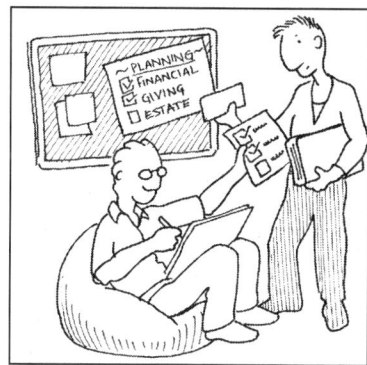

Enjoy the process! Like so much in this guide, the act of creating these plans will help you articulate your values more clearly to yourself and build into your relationship a foundation of listening, openness and trust.

## Spending plan

Whether you live on a budget or just spend as you please, tracking your expenses and then reflecting together on your separate or joint spending can be an illuminating values-clarification exercise as a couple. Even doing it for just a month or two can be useful.

> *For years, Roberto and Zack met in January to review their income and expenses of the past year and to evaluate how well their spending matched their values. They didn't need or want to live on a budget, but did appreciate this simple way to keep moving their spending choices in the direction of their values. Last year, they decided to eat out less and instead to use the money they saved to buy special groceries at Whole Foods and Trader Joe's. They also set a goal of doubling what they spend on gifts for friends.*

## Long-term financial plan

How much money do you actually need, individually and collectively, to feel secure long-term? How much can you feel free to spend? On what do you plan to spend it?

Making a long-term financial plan will give you both a much better picture of how much money you'll need for basic expenses and how much discretionary spending you can afford. You can make one plan for your joint lives or each have your own plan if most of your money is separate.

If this seems daunting, here are a few suggestions:

<u>Use the help of a fee-only certified financial planner.</u> The planner can help you create an initial plan, or if you are reasonably confident on the computer, you can draft a plan yourself on financial

planning/retirement planning software and then have a professional planner check your work. Having a financial plan on your own computer (instead of just the planner's computer) will enable you to play with parameters, try on different scenarios, and easily change your plan over time.

<u>Value the planning process</u>. Perhaps making a joint plan will be quick and easy for you. But don't be surprised if it raises feelings of anxiety, confusion, and values differences between you. Take the time you need to do it thoroughly and get to the bottom of what is important to both of you, but keep the process moving to completion.

<u>Expect to revise your financial plan</u> every few years, when major changes happen in your lives or in the economy. Any plan is simply a good guess. Then reality happens!

**Giving Plan**

Couples sometimes have very different beliefs and practices about giving, both the amounts to give and where the money should go. Should your "surplus" be put towards savings or towards giving? Should some level of giving continue no matter what your financial circumstances are? What causes do you each care about and why? What about gifts to family and friends in need? These questions can engender strong feelings and opinions. As we suggest in the "Money Histories" section, take time to thoroughly hear each other out, including the history of your values and beliefs, before trying to craft solutions.

Whether you decide to jointly make all of your giving choices, or to do some or all of your giving separately, we encourage you to work out multi-year, written giving plans. Include how much you intend to give per year (as a dollar amount, or percentage of income or assets), the methods and timing of your gifts, and the kinds of organizations or causes you want to support. You might include a "discretionary fund" of an amount for the year that you can each give spontaneously to things that move you (e.g. friends' pet projects, walk-a-thons, etc.).

Working together on your giving plans will not only help prevent future conflicts, but will help each of you be more conscious, effective, and satisfied in whatever giving you do. Some couples find giving together one of their most joyous activities.

**Estate Plan or Will**

If you don't have a will yet, either as individuals or as a couple, make one this week! Any will is better than none. Just sit and write a letter as if you were writing to a friend. Lawyers can then make it official. If your situation is simple enough, you can even just use an online template and get it notarized. You can always improve it, but get it done!

To whom do you want to leave your possessions …your financial assets? Remember, a will is written for the possibility that you might die tomorrow. You're not guessing about the future; you're making important decisions about your finances right now. It is a wonderful values clarification exercise for couples at any stage of being together. How much money will you leave to your children? Will any of your assets go to charity? You can learn a great deal about each other by talking through the many values questions involved in creating your wills.

Once the legal part is complete, you might write personal notes to loved ones explaining the thinking behind your decisions and expressing your love. These more informal letters can be referenced in your will or just filed where your executor (the person you name to implement the will) can find them.

# *Money: key points*

### Exchange money histories

Plan on several sessions
Explore many topics (in childhood, youth, adulthood)
Take turns and empathize
Discuss ways to build on strengths
Discuss ways to address limitations

### Address differences in power

Voice discontents
Recognize societal influences
Dialogue
Explore options
Experiment and evaluate

### Four ways to share money

Discuss whether and how to share:
- Expenses
- Management
- Decision-making
- Ownership

Sharing money is not all or nothing.

### Make written plans together

Spending plan
Long-term financial plan
Giving plan

# Parenting

How do most couples get along once they add all the intense demands of parenting? For ourselves, we relied heavily on all the skills described in the first section of this guide. Good thing we had nearly a decade to practice them before getting pregnant!

Throughout much of our son's early years, Christopher struggled with fathering and Anne struggled to affirm Christopher's contributions rather than add to his already ample self-criticism. The concepts and skills described in "Helping each other change" truly saved our relationship. The practice of slathering on praise as described above in the "Appreciations" section was essential in the early years and continues to give us nourishment now, as we parent our young adult son.

Below are a few of the additional skills and insights that helped us through the journey of parenting.

## Learn from role models

We learn a lot, consciously and unconsciously, by what we absorb of others' behavior. Take the time to discuss with your partner other couples you know as parents, to see what you can learn. It's great to do this kind of sharing at different stages of parenting (e.g., before you conceive, when children are small, when they are teens, and when they are young adults). Here are some exercises we found particularly helpful:

Exercise: Your parents' relationship
Share each of your observations of your own parents' relationship and how parenting seemed to affect them as a couple. Talk about how you experienced their relationship as a child and how you feel about it now. What would you wish to emulate in their relationship as parents and what would you like to do differently? What assumptions have you internalized about how couples parent together from the ways your mom and dad behaved?

Exercise:  Other couples you observed parenting
Name other couples you know you (including peers, friends of your parents, relatives) who parent together and whose relationships inspire you. Discuss what you would like to emulate as well as ways your preferences different.

## Negotiate big decisions

There are various big decisions about parenting. Probably the first one, the decision whether or not to have a child, is one of the biggest decisions many couples face. Although some people say "just go ahead and do it," if the two of you have fundamentally different expectations about parenting, these are likely to come back and bite you in the years ahead when you'll have little slack to talk them over.

Talk before you act. If your conversations uncover big differences, don't give up. Use the tools in this guide, especially the systematic decision-making model, to think creatively and negotiate how to maximize meeting different needs. Even when the needs may first appear to be irreconcilable, with ample motivation and creativity, workable solutions may emerge.

> *Marguerite: When I was 51% sure I wanted us to go ahead and conceive, my partner Tay still had major reservations. Despite the skinny margin of my leaning towards having children, I took to heart my mother's wisdom not to wait for a mythical "better time." So I actively pursued working it out with Tay.*
>
> *Tay: Marguerite and I met as activists, and I cherished that shared connection. Our social change work felt core to me and I was afraid that if we had a child, all our energy would go to parenting, instead. So we "cut a deal," that within three years of having a child we'd do some important work out in the world together, whether volunteer or paid.*

A negotiation could work in either of these directions: toward having children or deciding not to. Following is an example in the other direction.

*Nina: Jack and I have used the decision-making processes in this guide for years, including for how many children to have.*

*Jack: I was happy with our family of two daughters and didn't want the responsibility of more children. Yet, right after Nina's beloved mother died, Nina was seized with yearning for more children and the chance to add a boy to our family. Her mother's death reminded her again of how much she had loved growing up in a large family.*

*Nina: Again and again, we returned to the Systematic Decision-Making Process [described in chapter 3]. Finally, I realized that my leaning for more children was slight, flavored by ambivalence as well as yearning. Did I really want to go back to diapers? And even though I thought Jack's strong preference for a smaller family was colored by his own difficult childhood, collectively our leaning was clearly to stay with two children.*

*Jack: So we decided to stay with two children.*

## Respect differences

Parenting is filled with losses and major challenges. Many couples deal with fertility and birthing losses: struggles to conceive, miscarriage, abortion, stillbirth, the disappointment of having a C-section instead of vaginal birth. Over the course of a lifetime, parents deal together with innumerable parenting-related losses or challenges, whether from the injuries, illnesses, and disabilities of their children, or simply from the loss of cherished hopes they had for them.

Often, each person in the couple processes deep emotions differently. One person may take a lot more time than the other, may be more expressive, or may interpret circumstances differently. As a couple, one of the hardest and most important things you can do for your relationship is to accept the different ways each of you grieve.

*Our first child died in utero after a full nine months, just before Anne went into labor. Christopher's grief was a sudden rush,*

> bringing up the loss of his mom who had died when he was 14. But within weeks of the stillbirth, he was eager to move on and to absorb himself in work. In contrast, Anne's grief was sustained and physical; for months afterward, hard sobbing would overtake her without warning. The best thing we did for our relationship was to refrain from judging or blaming each other for our differences, and to each seek emotional support from other people (mostly, Christopher from other men and Anne from other women).

While the challenge of a loss is more obvious, the differences in experiencing parenting joys can be stressful for a couple. One parent may be delighted to attend every school play and recital, beaming with pride, while the other parent may find elementary school events too boring to tolerate.

Again, the key concept is to allow each person to parent in his or her own way, and to find new creative ways to meet the needs instead of getting snagged on judgments. For instance, in the above example, instead of feeling lonely and resentful, the parent who attends school plays could bring a loving friend as company, so they can beam together at the child. The parent who can't stand school recitals, instead of feeling judged as a bad parent, could find other ways to show the child her interest and involvement. Of course, the child's needs are also a key part of the equation and need to be thoughtfully considered too.

## Step out of limiting assumptions

We all make many assumptions, sometimes unconsciously, about what it means to be a good mother or a good father, and what it means to share the burdens and pleasures of parenting. If we're falling short of our own or our co-parent's expectations, what needs to change? Sometimes it's not our behavior but rather our assumptions.

> *Beth: When Angela and I chose to have a child via anonymous donor, we both were happy with me carrying the child. Yet after our daughter, Nikki, was born, Angela struggled to bond with her. This continued for years and was terribly hard on our relationship. I judged Angela for not just "snapping out of it" and for not getting therapy about her own distant and judgmental mom, since I assumed her history was affecting her ability to parent.*

> *Angela: Finally, after Nikki was about 10 years old, a light bulb went off in my head. I was distant to my own mom, but very close to both my grandmothers. What if I "retired from being mom" and instead imagined myself as my daughter's grandmother?!*

> *Beth: This wacky idea finally has proved to be the biggest breakthrough of our parenting relationship. Previously, I was the permissive and empathetic parent and Angela was the uptight limit-setter. When Angela became "a grandmother" she could let go of nagging (do your chores, finish homework, get to bed) and focus instead of doing playful and connective activities with our daughter, as well as offering support to me.*

> *Angela: So that's what we did. Beth took on 98% of the daily parenting work (which she said actually felt easier because she could do it by her standards alone). I taught Nikki tennis and waterskiing and took her to concerts. If I wanted to nudge Nikki to do something, I had to suggest it to Beth, and she could choose to make the nudge or not. From this radical shift in roles, Nikki's and my relationship slowly and steadily improved, even during all her teenage years, when many moms and daughters are at loggerheads.*

There are infinite ways to structure good parenting relationships, so long as they work for all concerned. The important thing is to be aware of what's working and what's not working, and experiment with shifting the roles to better meet everyone's needs.

Exercise: Thinking out-of-the-box
List what roles each of you play as parents. Then each rate your level of satisfaction with these roles (from 1-10, with 1 as very low and 10 as very high). Each of you pick one role that had a low rating and brainstorm creative ways to change what isn't working for you. Discuss your brainstorm ideas and choose one or more new ways to play your role. Agree on a period of time to experiment; then evaluate the results.

**So much more to say**

Every couple faces different challenges and joys as parents. We're keenly aware that we address here only a few of our own, rather idiosyncratic challenges, which may be different from yours. Divorced families, blended families, same-sex couples, couples where a parent or child is disabled, where children are adopted… all these circumstances put different stresses on couple relationships. We also limited our comments here to how couples can get along better as they parent, leaving aside the enormous realm of parenting skills. We have already described in earlier chapters all the skills we used get along together as parents. Thus, this section is brief, even though the challenges of parenting are vast.

# *Parenting: key points*

---

### Learn from role models

Talk about your parents and other couples
What do you want to emulate?
What do you want to do differently?

---

### Negotiate big differences

Use the Systematic Decision-making Process
Think creatively
Maximize meeting each person's needs

---

### Respect differences

Men and women often grieve differently
Get support from your own gender
Allow grief and joy to be expressed in your own ways
Meet needs rather than judge each other

---

### Step out of limiting assumptions
Examine the roles each of you play as parents
Consider out-of-the-box ways to meet needs

# Aging together

At this writing, both of us are 57 years old. We know age is relative: Anne's mother, currently 92, views us as in the prime of life, but compared to our past selves, we feel bizarrely old. Every day we're confronted by our aging bodies, spirits, and identities, and by how these affect our relationship. Sometimes we're shocked and frightened by the extent of our wrinkles and gray hair, aches and pains, greater fatigue, and by how these are likely (if we're lucky!) to increase as we get older. Aging—oy!

We're also enormously grateful. How incredible to have had 32 (thus far) years of life experience together! We're deeply contented and comfortable: cooking a meal together… curling up together for a short nap almost every day after lunch… exclaiming together over the beauty of the sunset. These ordinary moments are joys we don't take for granted.

Much of the time, we find this peaceful ease delicious. Yet, at other times, our daily familiarity feels dull and confining. In fact, at this middle-aged juncture, our relationship feels filled with age-related contradictions and crosscurrents:

> **Committed to continuity, yet craving change.** *Many couples separate at this age, especially as children leave home. We're committed to staying together and building on the goodness of our lives, yet we're also hungry to experience adventure, growth, and change.*
>
> **Thoroughly interdependent, yet desiring autonomy.** *Over the years, our possessions, finances, work, vacations, friendships, and memories have all become increasingly shared. Even though we have always supported each other's growth, we're aware we may be limiting each other by our togetherness. We've been moving toward greater autonomy and time away from each other, and suspect it would growthful to do so even more.*
>
> **Wonderfully secure, yet keenly vulnerable.** *More than ever, we're confident that we're together for life. However, along with*

> *this delicious security we feel keenly vulnerable. Disability or death might take either of us at any time. Friends our age and younger have already died.*

If you and your partner have been together for decades, perhaps you relate to these cross-currents, and like us, are dealing with the twin challenges of being together a long time plus becoming middle-aged or old in this culture. Below are a few of the ways we're taking these on.

## Renew your sexuality

Sooner or later, getting older confronts couples with the difference between past sexuality and current reality. Many feel uncomfortably disoriented by changed (and changing) bodies and declining response levels. It could be all-too-easy to take out feelings of loss on each other. Instead, it can be a good time to start new practices that remind each other you are allies, seeking to nurture your sexual connection as you become old. Here are a few practices that help us:

### Get perspective by looking back at the present

Pretend that you and your partner are in your late 90's (or at least 10 years older than you are now). Exclaim with amazement as you "look back" at how young and able-bodied you are now.

> *Johnny, wow, how few wrinkles are on your face! Look at how easily you can get into bed!*

### Mourn losses

Instead of trying to deny or minimize the sadness of pleasures lost, or leaping to "solve the problem," first join in and mourn the losses together with genuine and playful gusto.

> *Diane: Aargh, my orgasms are so elusive and mild compared to what they used to be!*
> *Brad: How sad and frustrating! No fair!*

## Praise the new looks

Most of us are terribly influenced by society's pervasive view of older people as unattractive, whether we intellectually believe it or not.

Whenever you can, offer genuine complimentary appreciations to counter your partner's negative self-image about looking old. Lay it on thick.

*Sam, I love your beautiful white chest hair. Your bald head looks sexy to me!*

## Notice gains

Take time to notice what new pleasures of sensuality and connecting are opening up as arousal is far slower to build, without the "swept away" rush of hormones or early romance.

> *Now that my partner and I need to engage our imagination more to get aroused, we're having a great time reading erotica and sharing fantasies—something we didn't bother with before.*

## Acknowledge even tiny irritations

Over the first decade of our relationship we became proficient at processing misunderstandings and conflicts between us, using the skills described in the first part of this guide. Taking the time to quickly clear up annoyances was a fundamental part of our relationship. We called it the "Clean Windshield Commitment": if you wash the squished bugs and dirt off your car windshield daily, you have a lovely clear view of the world; if instead you let the bug crust stay on, it gets mighty hard to wash off. Eventually you think it's normal to look at the world through a dirty film. We're proud to have kept the windshield of our relationship clean and have avoided the painful relationship 'car wrecks' we've seen of some other couples.

Yet as we've entered our third decade together, and as Anne is in the thick of menopause, a new relationship challenge has arisen. We both feel barraged by micro-irritations, our name for annoyances that often seem too minor or too imbedded in the other's personality to bring up. They are tiny things that the other person may have no clue that we now find irritating. Maybe it's the way Christopher only likes his coffee in a carefully prepared way, or the way Anne pauses frequently in her sentences. Little things that were fine with us in earlier years now feel grating.

It can be tempting to keep micro-irritations to yourself:

> *Oh, it's just my stupid hormones making me so picky and thin-skinned. Such mundane things really shouldn't bother me. I don't want my partner to feel picked on or to walk on eggshells around me.*

Since it's your own fault for being bothered, is it better to keep these petty annoyances to yourself? Don't be fooled. Unprocessed irritations, especially tiny and repetitive ones, can become like a low-grade infection, constantly souring how you feel with your beloved. It's the hiding of irritations that give them power; if they are allowed or even welcomed, much of the negative charge dissolves. Taking the time to learn from little annoyances (using the many skills from this guide) will help keep the air between you clear.

A few suggestions:

> *Be sure to ask, "Is this a good time to process a micro-irritation?" Don't just leap in!*
>
> *Follow the processes suggested in the "Step out of Upsets, section" including taking turns, empathizing, and "The Glitch Process."*
>
> *You might develop a non-verbal signal (e.g. tugging your ear-*

*lobe) to simply note that a micro-irritation has occurred. The other person nods to acknowledge the signal. Then you wait to discuss it when it's a good time and place. This is especially useful when at a restaurant with friends or other public place. Just the freedom to note it helps reduce the annoyance.*

*Even if processing micro-irritations is welcomed, the one receiving them can easily feel criticized. If irritations are frequent or one-sided, you might agree to save all processing for a pre-determined daily time when you both have good energy.*

*Be sure to balance the processing of irritations with exchanging lots of empathy and appreciations.*

Some micro-irritations really are just fluff—a mood, a passing phase, something that evaporates once expressed. Other micro-irritations contain hidden nuggets of gold to offer the relationship. They point to needs that aren't getting fulfilled and changes you can easily make to increase each other's happiness. Enjoy your treasure hunt!

## Question accommodation

In younger years, especially if you were juggling parenting or demanding careers, constant accommodation to each other's rhythms and needs may have seemed necessary.

As you age, these habitual accommodations may no longer be required or even tolerable. Especially for many menopausal women and empty-nesting mothers who spent a lifetime putting others' needs first, previously easy accommodations can feel to their nerves like the screech of fingernails on a blackboard. Have the two of you always gone to bed at the same time? Maybe it's time now to follow your own rhythms. When making daily decisions, has one of you usually gone along with the preferences of the other? Maybe that pattern no longer feels right. Relish the chance to look at old habits and decide anew.

## Don't settle for boredom

If you've been together a long time and have many comfortable routines, it's easy for a layer of boredom to coat the relationship. Below are a few of the ways the two of us are looking to bring greater variety and enlivenment into our times together. Perhaps you would like to try them, too.

### Small changes

Being inventive takes energy, something you may not always have. But as the documentary film "Happiness" revealed: even tiny differences in routines can add a surprising amount of zest to life. Think about small steps you can take: changing who sleeps on which side of the bed, who usually drives, what kind of music you listen to. Habits abound. Give them a jiggle.

### Surprise dates

Make a "surprise date" at least once a month. One partner creates the plan; the other has no idea about what's to come. Each date, alternate who takes the lead. In addition to regularly scheduled surprise dates, if some good opportunity comes up either of you can propose a new surprise date at a specified time.

During the date, the recipient is encouraged to cheerfully go along with whatever is planned, whether or not it's his cup of tea. (He can have veto power if he finds something truly objectionable.) Talking about what it's like to be in each role can be a valuable part of the date. What does it feel like to let go of control and be led? Is it relaxing? Scary? Fun? Like being a child? How about taking the lead? Does that feel powerful? Burdensome? Freeing? Experiencing different ways to follow or lead through having surprise dates can offer you a surprisingly rich amount to learn.

### Playing with characters

Customary habits can feel glued to you like tight costumes you have forgotten how to remove. Sometimes our very personalities, familiar and beloved as they are, feel tedious and tiresome. Yet to act differently from our norm can feel fake, a violation of being genuine.

Try shaking up rigid personas by taking on a character with different qualities than you usually manifest. For example:

> *Act out "disowned" or "shadow" parts. For instance, Dani is almost always kind and gentle. She is enjoying playing with a new persona she is calling "Bitch," who has an attitude, and is blunt or nasty.*
>
> *Act out desired qualities. For instance, Charles wishes he would more often be light and expressive rather than tired and anxious. He once decided to attend the opening night of an arts conference as "Zim," a character who is bursting with friendliness, curiosity, brazenness, and zest. He had a much better time than usual!*
>
> *Play with improvisation exercises where you assume unfamiliar characters, roles, and situations. For instance, talk in pretend foreign accents.*

Over time your characters might expand your repertoire of who you are, allow yourself to release uptightness, become more aware of shadow parts, develop more of your desired qualities, and have more fun.

## *Aging together: key points*

**Renew your sexuality**

Get perspective by looking back at the present
Praise the new looks
Mourn losses
Notice gains

**Acknowledge even tiny irritations**

Make the "Clean Windshield" commitment
Agree to address micro-irritations
Use the Glitch Process and other tools
Develop a nonverbal signal
Balance frequent processing with appreciations

**Question accommodation**
Now is the time to change old habits

**Don't settle for boredom**

Create small changes
Make surprise dates
Play with characters
 - disowned qualities
 - desired qualities
 - improvisation games

# Working Together

There are innumerable ways for couples to dedicate their combined energies towards "a greater purpose." Those who share a faith might fully participate together in their faith community; others who share political values might both campaign for candidates or attend rallies together. Some couples deliberately give to the world by building a loving home that serves as a welcoming haven. Many consider the raising of the next generation as the greatest purpose of their love. Whatever form it takes, there is beauty and meaning in knowing your love not only serves each other, but amplifies your ability to serve the wider community.

For us, working together as social entrepreneurs has served this purpose. Many couples are happy and fulfilled without combining their vocational lives. Yet for better or worse, jobs claim a major portion of most people's time. Sweethearts who can successfully join each other in paid work will likely spend more time together, and share more goals, challenges, and memories than couples that work separately.

> *Christopher: A life dream of mine was to work with a best friend. I gathering up my courage and propositioned Anne for us to work together.*
>
> *Anne: At first I thought, "Are you kidding?? We're both so insecure about work. We'll just drag each other down!" But 23 years later, I can say that joining our work lives has helped us stay together. Far more than other common "glues" among couples (e.g. parenting, sex, travel) working together has been a reliably profound and pleasurable aspect our relationship.*
>
> *Christopher: Because our work hasn't been mainly about making money, but about furthering causes to which we are fiercely dedicated, working together gives our love a deeper purpose. Together, we contribute something meaningful to the world – more effectively than either of us could do alone.*

Many couples fear that the stress and power dynamics of working together could choke all nurturance out of their relationship. In our first years of working together, we certainly spent a lot of time processing difficulties using all the skills in this guide. Over time, we upset each other less and enjoyed ourselves more. We also developed some new tools and concepts specific to the challenges of working together.

Below are a few tools you might find useful in your work relationship, even if the work you do together is the unpaid labor of running a household or parenting.

### Clarify decision-making roles

Many misunderstandings can be avoided by clarifying ahead of time who will be involved in making decisions and in what way. Whether you are part of a larger team or just working as a couple, gaining fluency with the roles below can be helpful.

Obviously, in situations where things work smoothly and organically you don't need to negotiate these roles. Unfortunately, even when you think you're clear, your partner (or others) may find the decision-making authority ambiguous or confused. That is where the model below can come in handy. While it was developed for decision-making in organizations, we've successfully used it for couples as illustrated by the examples here. (Read more in the "RAPID Decision-Making" article in the Resource section.)

**Decision maker:** Must be part of the decision.

> *For efficiency's sake, it's simplest to have just one of you make a decision. Yet for more complex or important decisions, you might want the wisdom that can come from both of you (or even a larger team) making the final decision together.*
>
> *Janis: "William, I know you were going to decide the agenda for meeting with Ms. K, but I realized I need to be part of the meeting too and want to decide the agenda with you."*

**Advisor:** Does not make the decision, but must give feedback at one or more clearly named points in the decision-making process.

If you play the role of Advisor you need to be asked for input early enough that you can suggest major changes in a timely way. (E.g., Ask your advisory partner for input on an article at least a week before a deadline, not the day before it is due for publication.) Make it clear whether your Advisor gives feedback once or multiple times, and ideally at what points in the process. The Advisor should clearly state which parts of her feedback she feels strongly about and which are more optional. The Decision-maker is not required to go along with all of the Advisor's recommendations, but if not, he may need to explain why.

> Zed: "Jim, I know I'm the decision-maker on this project, but could you advise me about how to make it more successful? I'd like to meet with you this week for the planning process and next week after I have a draft proposal done."

**Input-giver:** Is invited to give input by a specific date/time, but is not required to.

This difference between the Advisor (who is expected to respond to requests for feedback) versus an Input-giver (whose feedback is optional) is especially important in a larger team, when waiting for many responses can slow a project.

> Doris: "Liu, if you want to give me input on one or two additional people I should visit on this work trip to San Francisco, please give me their names by Tuesday at noon. If I don't hear from you I'll just settle the schedule myself."

**Manager:** Is responsible to move the decision to completion by a certain date.

Often the Manager of a decision is also Decision-maker. But this role can be delegated to someone else since simply moving a decision along can be a substantial organizing task in a big team.

124 | Getting Along

Even as a couple, it can be helpful to state who will manage the decision.

> *Eleanor: "Mark, we need to decide together by Friday whether we're going to write that fundraising letter of inquiry. I'm flat out with meetings the next two days. Would you be willing to manage this decision so we don't miss the deadline?"*

## Negotiate communication preferences

Sometimes modest differences in communication styles can make the difference between getting along and driving each other crazy. Identifying key differences and making agreements about them—making it clear that no style is inherently "right" or "wrong"—can foster greater ease and harmony. Two examples:

### Punch line versus story

Some people strongly prefer to hear the punch line or conclusion, without a lead-in story. Hearing the long version drives them wild with impatience to get back to work. Others enjoy the free expression of a longer story and the chance to vent feelings, as well as the pleasure of socializing, and find the punch line version unfriendly and constraining.

Punch line version:
> *Billy exclaims, "The printer is jammed. Can you help me?*

Story version:
> *Billy exclaims: "I got up so early this morning to work on that important grant proposal I've been sweating over all month. In fact, it is due by 5pm today. Everything was going really well, but when I tried printing the three charts at the end of the proposal the first two pages came out fine, but then something happened*

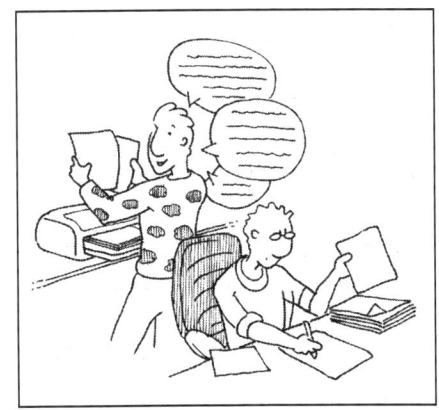

*and the paper jammed. If I don't get this done on time, Jack will be really upset. Can you help?"*

If you've talked about the differences, you can make agreements. For instance, anyone can say gently, "Punch line, please" and the others will understand the request. And those who enjoy longer versions can happily tell longer versions to each other. Or you can negotiate, "George, the punch line is that Melissa and I just had another big fight. I'm really upset and need to talk about what happened. Do you have some time right now?"

## Interruptions

Some people prefer a work environment with lots of easy give-and-take. Why work together if you're not going to interact? Others really need quiet to keep their focus.

Those who tend to interrupt can learn to ask, "Could I ask you a quick question?" or "Would you have time today to help me think about something for five minutes?" instead of just launching in.

Those who prefer quiet focus can suggest regular times that work for interaction. "How about you save your questions, and every day after lunch we'll take 15 min. to go over them?" or "I could hold Thursday mornings as times when we talk together as we work. Would you like that?"

## Offer feedback or advice skillfully

In theory, most of us value receiving personal feedback about our own performance or behavior, yet being offered advice unsolicited can sometimes feel like being scolded, patronized, or micromanaged. Even when we've asked for input, it's easy to get defensive. Here is a process that helps feedback sessions be more useful and friendly:

### Check whether feedback is desired and when.

*Shirley, would you like feedback on your facilitation of today's meeting? Yes? Would you prefer it now, or would some other time be better?*

**Clarify the process.**

*Would you first like to tell me your own assessment? Or would you like to hear my feedback first?*

**Be specific and concise.**

*I'd like to tell you 3 things I liked that you did and 1-2 suggestions. How does that sound? (Offer more affirmation than constructive criticism.)*

**Be ready to listen to feelings.**

*You sound upset. Would you like to vent for a minute about how frustrating it was, before I say any more?*

**Help the recipient digest your feedback.**

*Was any of that useful to you? Do you have any questions about my suggestions?*

## Nurture the relationship

Even if your work is inherently rewarding, the constant pressures and demands of work can erode the sweetness of a relationship (especially if it's on top of the demands of running a household and/or raising children). Also, if you're together nearly all the time, it may be hard to feel that lovely hunger for each other's company. To protect and regularly feed the pleasure of being together, you can develop rituals in three categories: boundaries, nourishment, and intimacies.

### Boundaries on work time

Because work can expand to fill every moment given it, mutually agree upon some limits. For example:

> *- No work conversations before 9am or after 9pm.*
> *- No work conversations during family time, dates or lovemaking.*
> *- No venting about anything work-related that implicates the other person, unless you clearly forewarn your partner that the rant might trigger them, and then get their OK to proceed.*
> *- Schedule time apart from each other (e.g., one day a week; one weekend a season).*

## Nourishment

If you work at home or have control over your work environment, take advantage of it. Use the freedom to develop rituals that nourish your relationship. These nourishing rituals can include and benefit other staff as well. For example:

> *Cook and eat special lunches together.*
> *Put on favorite soothing or energizing music when working.*
> *Put on a favorite dance song and take a dance break.*

## Intimacies

So long as you are respectful of others around you, you don't need to act like "normal" co-workers do. You can harness the healing power of your closeness to have a better workday. For example, especially if you work at home, you can:

> *Briefly nap or meditate together after lunch.*
> *Have difficult work conversations lying in each other's arms.*
> *When no one is around, surprise your partner with a kiss.*

### Introduce new initiatives carefully

Couples that work together, especially in their own business or as entrepreneurs, can easily become polarized when one person tends to be visionary and the other pragmatic. In that painful dance, the Visionary feels her creativity is squashed because the Pragmatist responds with anxiety when any new idea is proposed. "Why are you already scowling? I've barely let the words out of my mouth!" The Pragmatist resents being cast as the bad guy, when he is just trying to be realistic and keep the team from getting overwhelmed. "How can you suggest a big new project now? You know we have no money to hire more staff!"

Here is a process for considering new ideas that can cut through this polarity and help both sides relax. Even when couples (or groups) are not polarizing, they may find this process helpful.

### Step 1: Contract for time to raise a new possibility

Rather than blurting out his new ideas and expecting excited response, the Visionary carefully helps the Pragmatist be ready to hear his thoughts. "I've got a new idea I'd like to explore. It's not a proposal. I don't know if I'd want us to do it. But I want some receptive space to explore it together. Is now a good time?"

### Step 2: Acknowledge context and generate ideas

First, the Visionary briefly acknowledges any prior relevant context or agreements. ("I know we've said we don't want to supervise more workers.") Then, he encourages the Pragmatist to put her anxiety aside, to ask open-ended questions, and to make whatever positive comments she genuinely can. No negative comments or concerns are expressed at this stage; all ideas are welcomed, no matter how wacky.

### Step 3: Name concerns

Now the Pragmatist and Visionary can both name concerns about the idea. Often misunderstandings are revealed in the discussion. ("Oh, I thought you meant...!") What would be needed to address the concerns? If both parties then agree the idea seems worth seriously considering, go on to the next phase. If not, hopefully you've at least had a constructive and amiable conversation instead of a fight.

### Step 4: Flesh out a proposal

If the idea is worth seriously considering, take time to spell it out in enough detail so that it can be more fully evaluated. This might be a process over days or weeks. Do whatever research is needed in order to propose in writing the goals, budget, and work plan.

## Step 5: Address concerns

Again, let both the Visionary and Pragmatist look at the proposal and discuss together how to address concerns. Ideally, get input from others.

## Step 6: Decide

Make a decision whether or not to move the initiative into implementation. Remember, at any stage, the idea can be acknowledged for its potential value and then shelved or released.

This process is useful not only in working together, but for any of the innumerable large work commitments couples take on together: renovating a home, having another child, living a year abroad... It can be useful instead of or in addition to the Decision-Making Process (earlier in this guide) whenever a decision being considered would generate a good deal of work for both parties.

### Build on strengths and address limitations

In any good work team, members usually get to know each other's strengths and weaknesses and divide the work accordingly. But when couples work together, divisions of labor can become touchy. The less competent partner (in a given area) may feel embarrassed, abandoned, or judged; the more competent partner (in a given area) may feel burdened, frustrated, and resentful. These differences may get further aggravated through gender roles and patterns, as well as with tensions you experience outside the workplace.

It can help to explore this with gentle awareness. See if you can come to agreement about each other's different strengths and limitations. Make a conscious decision together about when you'll build on existing strengths, and when and how to address limitations.

> *Jill has a history of writing block and freezes on first drafts. Yet she is a competent editor once a draft is written. Jill happily agreed to have her partner Samantha write all the first drafts, and she is gaining writing confidence by being the editor.*
>
> *Billy is "good at guy things" such as fixing office equipment, dealing with the computer, and managing the project finances. So without discussion, he slipped into those roles. Once they discussed it, he and his partner Sarah agreed that she'd take the finances off his shoulder: she could feel more empowered and he become less burdened. Billy still is the main point person for the technology.*
>
> *Both Elsa and Robert avoid making the desperately needed sales calls, so finally they hired a sales manager, Melissa, who delights in that work.*

The book *Move to Greatness* describes four types of leadership energy needed for effective projects and organizations: (1) organizer, (2) visionary, (3) driver, and (4) collaborator. Ideally, everyone develops all four competencies, but of course each person has natural strengths and weaknesses.

We find this model easier to communicate to a team than the better-known and also useful Myers-Briggs or Enneagram personality models. As a couple in leadership, attending to these four qualities has helped us appreciate our individual qualities and to bring in other team members to build a full complement of different strengths.

> *Christopher's strong visionary energy is fortunately complemented by Anne's strong organizer energy. Christopher has great driver energy, and Anne is learning from him how to move a project forward. They both have strong collaborator energy with people they enjoy, but Christopher wants to become a better collaborator in situations where there is a less easy stylistic match with teammates.*

## Face the complications of co-leading as a couple

Sometimes being part of a couple that is leading an organization or a team can make things easier for you. When one of you wakes up at 3am with an anxiety attack, the other is already fully briefed for the ad hoc emergency strategy session! You can provide each other with a level of support, both emotional and practical, that would be impossible if you didn't both know each other and the work so well.

However, there can be complications that bite you. These are especially nasty if you're caught unaware, so here are a few of touchy issues to keep an eye out for:

**Parental projection:** Especially if you are a man and a woman running the show, your staff, clients, board members, and other stakeholders may see you as Mom and Dad. And this is especially difficult if they have had problematic relationships with either or both parents.

**Assumptions about communication:** Your team members may assume that if they have spoken to one of you, the other will be told about it, which may not necessarily be the case.

**Complaints or playing one off the other:** If team members find one of you more accommodating or easier to negotiate with, they may avoid the other or complain about him to you, rather than going directly to him to work things out.

When you catch dynamics like any of the above, take them seriously. Discuss them first with each other and then with your team. Know it may take many conversations to shift these patterns.

# *Working together: key points*

### Clarify decision-making roles

Decision-maker
Advisor
Input-giver
Manager

*- from Jon Huggett and Caitrin Moran, RAPID Decision-Making*

### Negotiate communication preferences

Talk about differences of style. For example:
- prefer punch line versus prefer full story
- prefer boundary versus prefer easy exchange

### Offer feedback or advice skillfully

Check if and when feedback is desired
Clarify the process
Be specific and concise
Offer more affirmation than criticism
Be ready to listen to feelings
Help the recipient digest your feedback

### Nurture the relationship

Make boundaries on work time
Add nourishment to your work day
Be energized by intimacies

### Introduce new initiatives carefully

1. Contract for time to raise a new possibility
2. Acknowledge the context and generate ideas
3. Discuss concerns
4. Flesh out a proposal
5. Address concerns
6. Decide whether to implement the new initiative

### Build on strengths and address limitations

Balance the four types of leadership energy:
    Visionary
    Organizer
    Driver
    Collaborator

*- from Ginny Whitelaw and Betsy Wetzig, Move To Greatness*

### Face the complications of co-leading

Parental projections
Assumptions about communication
Playing one off the other

# Closing

We relied heavily on the tools in this book to get along with each other through this big writing project. Many times the stress of writing together (on top of other demands) triggered old patterns and irritations—just so we don't get too smug! We needed every skill: taking turns... interrupting patterns... exchanging empathy and appreciation... and we must have used "the glitch process" dozens of times.

The tools came alive for us. We were not only re-inspired by their usefulness, but also recognized freshly where we needed to add more nuances to the older text. We also felt humbled by the places where we have yet to hone our own mastery.

Despite these glitches, our pleasure at co-creation far outweighed the annoyances. What could be more satisfying than working shoulder-to-shoulder with someone you love, creating a gift of value to others? For us it is only possible to pull this off because we integrate strong communication skills into our relationship.

## Reflect for connection

And so, our learning continues and we trust the same is true for you. At the beginning of the book we described four skill-learning stages that help us relax into the confusion and awkwardness of trying new skills. In closing we'd like to offer another generically useful tool we created to support our learning: a reflection process. Why not try it now, to reflect on your experience reading this guide?

Current education theory suggests that learning comes from a cycle of experience and reflection. An optimal ratio of reflection to experience is at least two to one. Yet many of us live such pressured lives we give little time to reflect on more than even a small fraction of the many experiences in our typical day.

Taking time to reflect daily on your life, even briefly, can help you to release tensions (before they accumulate in your internal organs and do damage), to learn from your life experience, and to be more in touch with yourself and with your partner.

We developed this model below to do satisfying reflection together in just 15-20 minutes. Although it is simple it has been so valuable to us that we use it nearly every day. Take turns with each question.

---

**Reflection process**

**Highlights:**
What are three things you enjoyed?

**Accomplishments:**
What are two things you are proud of?

**Challenge:**
Name one thing that was hard for you.
What's a lesson you take from it?

**Appreciation:**
Name something you're grateful for in your life or in your relationship.

---

We use this simple reflection format all the time to savor our experience and to highlight learning: when we're alone writing in our journals, when we're traveling and have just a few minutes on the phone together in which to get connected, at birthday dinners to reflect on the past year, and nightly, when one of us turns to the other before sleep and launches in: "What are three highlights of your day?"

## Be in touch

We've surprised ourselves with how much pleasure we got from writing down the tools in this guide and are excited to share them with you. Please adapt them to be more useful to you. Share the guide or any portion of it with your friends and loved ones.

Check out the website www.GettingAlong.Us to learn about what we're cooking up next or to reach us. We'd be delighted to hear from you about your experience in using any of tools. We offer phone or in-person consultations, workshops, and Playback Theatre performances on relationship themes (using improvisational theatre for empathy and appreciation of true stories people share from their lives). Invite us to visit!

With gratitude for all those who make love a skillful practice,

Anne and Christopher
Still on the trapeze, 2013

# Resources

## Communication and personal growth skills

Cameron-Bandler, Leslie. (1985) *Solutions: Practical and Effective Antidotes for Sexual and Relationship Problems.* San Rafael, CA: FuturePace, Inc.. Detailed description of approaches from neuro-linguistic programming applied to couples therapy.

Carson, Richard D. (2003) *Taming Your Gremlin.* New York: Quill. An amusing and profound book on how to love yourself.

Gordon, Thomas. (2001) *Leader Effectiveness Training.* New York, Perigee Trade. An invaluable set of skills for listening, assertiveness and problem-solving, applicable to everyone.

Hendrix, Harville. (2007) *Getting the Love You Want.* New York: Harper and Row. A marvelously wise guide to working through the obstacles to a partnership that works. Contains many valuable exercises.

Madson, Patricia Ryan. (2010) *Improv Wisdom: Don't Prepare, Just Show Up.* New York: Random House. A clear, concise book of key principles of improvisations, useful to everyday life.

Re-evaluation co-counseling (also called "RC"): A world-wide network providing peer counseling. One 16-week class provides a lifetime of essential emotional literacy. Don't be scared off by the organizational rigidity and weird jargon. Take what's useful and leave behind the rest. See: www.RC.org

Rosenberg, Marshall. (2003) *A Model for Nonviolent Communication.* Philadelphia: New Society Publishers. A short exercise book to help develop simple but potent communication skills for resolving conflict. Nonviolent communications workshops are offered online and world-wide. See: www.CNVC.org

## Sexuality

Brauer, Alan P. and Brauer, Donna J. (April 2001). *ESO: How You and Your Lover Can Give Each Other Hours of Extended Sexual Orgasm.* In addition to the orgasm tips, this book includes great exercises for releasing resentments increasing communication.

Daedone, Nicole. (May 2012) *Slow Sex.* Grand Central Life & Style. Describes a surprisingly powerful 15-minute practice of "orgasmic meditation" to enhance sexual ease and connection.

Deida, David. (March 2006). *The Way of the Superior Man: A Spiritual Guide to Mastering the Challenges of Women, Work, and Sexual Desire.* Controversial and thought-provoking.

Easton, Dossie and Hardy, Janet W. (March 2009). *The Ethical Slut: A Practical Guide to Polyamory, Open Relationships & Other Adventures.* A landmark book about exploring conscious, respectful, non-monogamous relationships.

Gass, Robert and Ansara, Judith. Wise and skillful trainers whose retreat for long-time couples made a difference in our relationship. See: http://sacredunion.com/couples/deepening-in-love/

Love, Patricia Love and Robinson, Jo. (June 2012). *Hot Monogamy: Essential Steps to More Passionate, Intimate Lovemaking.* A thorough, practical, fun guide for long-term relationships, whether monogamous or not.

Singer, Katie (April 2004). *The Garden of Fertility: A Guide to Charting Your Fertility Signals to Prevent or Achieve Pregnancy—Naturally...* Not to be confused with "the rhythm method," this fully reliable method also increases self-knowledge and communication.

Taylor, Patrica. (November 2001). *Expanded Orgasm: Soar to Ecstasy at Your Lover's Every Touch.* Naperville, Illinois: Sourcebooks Casablanca. Despite the hokey title, a mind-opening book about being fully present rather than goal-oriented during sex.

Resources | 141

## Money

*The Bolder Giving Workbook*: includes a simple one-page template for a giving plan and references to more sophisticated giving plan advice. Free download available at www.BolderGiving.org

Collins, Victoria. (1997). *Couples and Money*: Encino, CA: Gabriel Publications. A very readable guide with simple tools to help couples manage their finances and their relationship.

Leondar-Wright, Betsy. (2005). *Class Matters: Cross-class Alliance-Building for Middle Class Activists*. New Society Publishers. Full of stories, photos, cartoons, and tips on how work well with people of different class backgrounds.

Mellan, Olivia and Christie, Sherry. (2013). *Money Harmony: A Road Map for Individuals and Couples*. Money Harmony Books. Smart models and exercises to help couples navigate differences.

*More than Money* Journal: 43 issues of the journal available for free download. Full of stories and practical wisdom on how to put our money and values together. Look especially at the issues on Money and Couples (#5), Cross-Class Relationships (#17), and Money and Relationships (#40). See: MoreThanMoney.org.

Robin, Vicki. (2008). *Your Money or Your Life*. Penguin Books. An out-of-the-box roadmap of how to retire from money-making sooner rather than later, simplify your life, and focus on realizing your greatest gifts.

## Parenting together

Markova, Dawna with Powell, Annie. (1996). *How Your Child is Smart: A Life-Changing Approach to Learning*. Conari Press. A sophisticated model explaining visual, kinesthetic and auditory learning styles, useful for couples as well as parents.

RC family work: Browse the literature at www.rationalisland.com (search for "family" or "parenting").

## Working together

Huggett, Jon and Moran, Caitrin. (2008) Bridgespan Group article "RAPID Decision-Making: What it is, why we like it, and how to get the most out of it." A simple but powerful model of different key roles for decision-making. It's downloadable for free on the Social Enterprise Alliance Knowledge Center website.

Hanson, Birgit Zacher and Hanson, Tom (August 2010). *Who Will Do What by When?* Power Publications. A simple guide to a critical practical need.

Hawley, Miriam (Author), with McIntyre, Jeffrey (Aug 21, 2012). *You & Your Partner, Inc.: Entrepreneurial Couples Succeeding in Business, Life and Love.* Enlignment Inc. Interviews and insights from many couples who have worked together.

Stewart-Gross, Becky L. and Gross, Michael J. (July 2007). *Sleeping with Your Business Partner: A Communication Toolkit for Couples in Business Together.* Capital books. Offers many tips on improving communication and teamwork.

Whitelaw, Ginny and Wetzig, Betsy (Dec 4, 2007). *Move to Greatness: Focusing the Four Essential Energies of a Whole and Balanced Leader.* Nicholas Brealey. Offers images and movement exercises to strengthen leadership energies in an interesting model.

**We hope you get in touch with us!**

Give us feedback on this book. Share your own best practices and important lessons. Invite us to support your relationship.

Go to the website: **GettingAlong.Us**

Made in the USA
Charleston, SC
22 November 2013